TWINS
DOUBLE TROUBLE, DOUBLE TREAT

ANNIE GIBBINS

Copyright © Annie Gibbins

First published in Australia in 2022
by KMD Books
Waikiki, WA 6169

All rights reserved. No part of this book may be used or reproduced by any means, graphic, electronic, or mechanical, including photocopying, recording, taping or by any information storage retrieval system without the written permission of the copyright owner except in the case of brief quotations embodied in critical articles and reviews.

Because of the dynamic nature of the Internet, any web addresses or links contained in this book may have changed since publication and may no longer be vaild. The views expressed in this work are solely those of the author and do not necessarily reflect the views of the publisher and the publisher hereby disclaims any responsibility for them.

Edited by Eleanor Narey
Typeset by Dylan Ingram
Proofread by Chelsea Wilcox

 A catalogue record for this work is available from the National Library of Australia

National Library of Australia Catalogue-in-Publication data:

TWINS/Annie Gibbins

ISBN:
978-0-6454663-6-2
(Paperback)

ISBN:
978-0-6454663-7-9
(Ebook)

Birthing matters.
Your birthing experience matters.
Your children matter.
You matter.

*A real-life story to help you navigate
what comes next.*

*With love,
Annie and James Gibbins
Parents of five, including two sets of twins*

DEDICATION

This book is for all women, their partners and the communities that surround them. If you are pregnant with twins, have had twins, know twins or are a twin, I wrote this book for you.

My hope is that when you walk away from reading this, you will believe that you are capable of carrying, birthing and raising twins. But more importantly, that you are not alone. There are loving people around the world who are honorary members of your support system.

You can do this, and we are here for you.

Welcome to the family!

Disclaimer: I am a woman who was twice blessed with twins and then with another single birth. I cannot offer any medical advice, I'm not a doctor, a midwife or a doula, but I have run the gamut of experiences and earned my stripes within the community of mothers who have travelled the well-worn path of pregnancy, childbirth and raising twins.

GRATITUDE

I am a passionate and purpose-driven 'fempreneur' – global women's empowerment coach, CEO, podcast host, speaker and number-one bestselling author.

And I am also the immensely proud mother to my five children. This book is the product of love. I wouldn't be the woman I am today without the journey I have been on as a woman, wife and mum.

I am extremely grateful for our dear friends and family who have positively supported us through 32 years of unpredictable joy, challenges, triumphs, growth and blessings. You are the wings that helped us fly through storms. Because of your kindness and generosity, we not only survived, but thrived.

To my darling husband James, your love and support is heartfelt and cherished daily.

To my children Caleb, Daniel, Hannah, Samuel and Chelsea, you make me laugh, cry and definitely keep me real.

I love you all unconditionally.

Annie Gibbins

CONTENTS

PROLOGUE... 1
ENDORSEMENT 5

CHAPTER 1
TWO HEARTBEATS..8

CHAPTER 2
TWINS FACTS... 17

CHAPTER 3
THE PREGNANCY JOURNEY BEGINS...22

CHAPTER 4
LIFE DURING PREGNANCY 33

CHAPTER 5
PREPARING FOR BIRTH 50

CHAPTER 6
IT'S TIME TO DELIVER 64

CHAPTER 7
WHAT HAPPENS NEXT 70

CHAPTER 8
TWIN FEEDING 74

CHAPTER 9
PREPARING TO GO HOME... 77

CHAPTER 10
REMEMBER THE ENVIRONMENT... 87

CHAPTER 11
SELF-CARE IS ESSENTIAL 92

CHAPTER 12
ESTABLISHING A ROUTINE... 99

CHAPTER 13
LET GO OF PERFECTION... 101

CHAPTER 14
THE TEAM EFFORT 108

CHAPTER 15
POSTPARTUM BLUES.. 117

CHAPTER 16
TWIN DADS 122

CHAPTER 17
BEWARE OF SUPERMUM 129

CHAPTER 18
FREQUENT FAUX PAS 137

CHAPTER 19
DOUBLE TROUBLE 144

CHAPTER 20
INDIVIDUAL THOUGH BORN TOGETHER 149

CHAPTER 21
JUGGLING BABIES AND DREAMS 158

CHAPTER 22
IT'S FUNNY NOW 164

CHAPTER 23
LEARNED WISDOM 170

APPENDIX 1
STANDARD OBSTETRIC APPOINTMENT SCHEDULE 173

APPENDIX 2
NEW BABY CHECKLIST 178

APPENDIX 3
BIRTH PLAN TEMPLATE 181

APPENDIX 4
SAFETY CHECKLIST 186

ABOUT THE AUTHOR 190
REFERENCES 194

PROLOGUE

'Being a mother of twins is learning about strengths you didn't know you had and dealing with fears you didn't know existed.'
Annie Gibbins

In 1990, James and I were living in a tiny one-bedroom apartment in the seaside suburb of Manly. Raised on the Northern Beaches of Sydney, Australia, we both loved being surrounded by surf, sand and sunshine, so it was the perfect place to enjoy the first two and a half years of married life together. We were newlyweds, besotted with each other, and life was uncomplicated, fun and relaxed.

While our flat was dark and had issues with rising damp, it was conveniently located just a few minutes from the beach, which made us happy. James rode his bike back and forth to work at the local optometrist, enjoyed daily surfs during his lunchbreak and loved eating out, watching bands play live and playing soccer with his mates on the weekends. I commuted to Royal North Shore Hospital where I worked as a registered nurse and then spent my days off seeing friends, riding my bike around the neighbourhood and getting a golden tan as I watched my gorgeous husband surf.

Around work, our life was filled with beach days, bike riding and hanging out with friends. The honeymoon phase was still in full throttle. Besides our complex health problems and limited budget, life was darn near perfect, and we were not complaining.

I had suffered life-threatening asthma since I was 13 which activated when I exercised, laughed, got stressed or inhaled cold air. A simple jog down to the beach could leave me wheezing and struggling for breath – and on more than one occasion, a trip to the emergency unit. I hated being asthmatic as it seriously restricted my ability to engage in sport and made me say *'c'est la vie'* to the rocking bikini body I envied.

James was anaphylactic to all nuts, especially peanuts. Back then, no-one really understood nut allergies and labelling was poor. He was often referred to as a fussy eater. So, we implemented a nut-free household, navigated the occasional dining out by having direct conversations with the chef and prayed no-one accidentally poisoned him by contaminating his food. While this strategy definitely reduced the volume of EpiPens used over the years, the number of accidental exposures have been significant and cause my heart to skip a beat just thinking about each and every one of them.

From the moment we married, both in our early 20s, I chatted incessantly about how awesome it would be to have four daughters, two years apart, and the sooner we got cracking on having our gorgeous brood the better. Poor James. I have always been a highly energetic and passionate woman and it must have been exhausting at times listening to all my grand plans. James preferred to wait five years and felt three children of any gender would be more than enough to love, manage and finance.

And so, it was agreed that baby number one, boy or girl, should be planned somewhere in the middle. This new pattern of natural compromise was something that would become the norm for us as we journeyed through life together, and not just with each other.

The day arrived when I missed my period.

I was 100% distracted by what it could mean. I was at work, kept popping into the bathroom to check and recheck that my pad was still clean, and as soon as I had my break, I headed down to the pharmacy to purchase a pregnancy test. As I watched the two lines turn blue, I started jumping for joy in the loo. Pregnancy test in hand, I raced out to the nurses' station and asked my colleagues to confirm: I was indeed pregnant.

I was supported by a resounding, 'Wow! Oh my gosh! YES!'

I rang my beloved husband and told him the news that we were going to become parents. He was thrilled but also a bit nervous, to be honest with you.

Three weeks later, I was doubled over with cramps and bleeding, and sadly, I was going through a miscarriage. I was so shocked and devastated. I cried my eyes out for days. For whatever reason, this baby was not meant to be.

Two months later, we were anxious and excited when my pregnancy test was positive yet again. Over the next few weeks, I got used to waking up with extreme nausea, and if I smelt eggs, meat or coffee, it would trigger an intense bout of vomiting. While my excitement level was still sky-high, spending the next two months staring down the toilet bowl was a hard place to start our next chapter together. This time, we waited 12 weeks to tell our family and friends. Life was once again dreamy. We had no idea of the 'double treat' we were about to be blessed with!

ENDORSEMENT

Motherhood, at the best of times, is a combination of immense joy and constant challenge.

As an obstetrician, mum and personal friend of Annie's, my mind boggles at the thought of how she and James managed when they exploded into parenthood in their early 20s by having two sets of twins in 26 months!

While the visual image of a double pram PLUS a toddler at each side would overwhelm most parents of singletons, Annie speaks of it in the most natural way. After all, it was her daily reality and a necessity in the years pre-internet while James was at work.

According to the Australian Bureau of Statistics data 2017, in Australia, twins represent about 1.4% of all births, with an overall increasing trend in multiple births over the past two decades due to maternal age and use of assisted reproductive treatments. Twin pregnancy rates are also influenced by family history and ethnic background, however, sometimes, like the Gibbins found, they just surprise us.

As an obstetrician, multiple pregnancies mean a higher-risk

pregnancy. Starting from the ultrasound-based triage into identical (monozygotic) or fraternal (dizygotic) types, additional monitoring is highly recommended to ensure any presenting risks are minimised. For example, mothers of twins do carry an increased chance of gestational diabetes, high blood pressure, anaemia, caesareans and bleeding after delivery. There is also the raised potential for postnatal depression, so additional support should be planned for and assistance offered as appropriate.

Although 50% of twins are born prematurely (before 37 weeks of pregnancy) and babies are more likely to be of low birth weight for gestational age, significant medical advances in caring for neonates has meant better support for and survival of these babies. I am so glad that Annie is sharing her story. There is value in sharing tips and experiences around how they coped as a family, raised their amazing children, how she pursued her heartfelt professional dreams and vision, and frankly, stayed sane throughout the journey.

Every woman has a road map of what she wants out of life, and that individual plan may be a combination of personal, motherhood-based or professional goals. The good thing about reading a book where someone inspirational, like Annie, candidly communicates about the high and low points of her story is that I am hoping that women and their families will identify with her, appreciate the overall positivity and gain hope from the happy endings made so from her strength, struggle and resilience.

When I first met Annie, she was the CEO of the Australasian Society of Ultrasound in Medicine, and even with a social conversation, I felt that if she could be that successful whilst juggling five children, family and work, then so could I. I hope that same can-do energy comes to all who read this book!

Dr Talat Uppal MBBS, FRANZCOG DDU FSCHSM
Director, Women's Health Road, Australia

CHAPTER 1

TWO HEARTBEATS

'Twice the blessing, twice the fun. Two gorgeous miracles instead of one!'
Annie Gibbins

During my first obstetric appointment, I had to get 'comfortable' with the new routine of having internal and external 'up-close-and-personal' inspections of my vagina and uterus.

Apparently, all was 'just wonderful', albeit a little further along than expected, according to the obstetrician's measurements. This surprised me as I was sure my dates were correct but, hey, *he* was the doctor! After leaving my appointment, I headed straight to the local shopping mall and purchased a baby book and some dry biscuits to help curb my 'all-day' morning sickness.

When the blood test results came back 'showing some irregularities', my doctor referred me for my three-month ultrasound, or as some of us call it a sonogram or baby scan. This was an exciting time for James and me, and we couldn't wait to hear our little baby's heart beating and to get a blurry picture to put on our fridge. My excitement level had flicked into turbocharge!

TWINS

Being a nurse, I knew drinking water before an ultrasound results in a clearer picture. Wanting the best results, I got to drinking one glass, two glasses, three glasses, four; I was one very determined and focused mama. As I lay on the table with my bladder filled to the brim, the sonographer started scanning and even let me take a quick break to let out some water. I had taken the 'fill your bladder concept' too far and couldn't lay still. As she continued scanning and started clicking buttons on her machine, she looked at us and said, 'Baby One has a strong heartbeat and so does Baby Two! Your dates are correct. You are having twins.'

We were having twins!

'Did you just say *twins?*' James asked.

'Yes, you are definitely having twins, and they both look healthy,' she said.

As she continued scanning and labelling the mixture of body parts, which all looked unidentifiable to us, we spent the time staring at the screen, grinning at each other and trying to process this news. We requested not to be told the genders as we wanted to keep that a surprise for the birth.

For some bizarre reason, I assumed they would both be girls. I have no idea why but maybe, after being raised with two brothers, I subconsciously wanted to create a home filled with more oestrogen and less testosterone to enjoy in my older years. With the giddiness and excitement of being told we were having twins, we floated out of the hospital, went for coffee and realised that we hadn't asked any meaningful questions whatsoever. All of a sudden, our minds were flooded with things we should have asked!

- Can you tell if they are identical or fraternal?
- Will their due date change?
- What do we do next?

When we returned home, we kissed, hugged, laughed and commenced exploring how this exciting news would impact our lives. Considering we lived in a one-bedroom unit, owned an old car and had little cash, we assumed it would be significant, just not sure how. Trust 'us two' to be having twins!

We were a couple who never did anything by halves and were always setting ourselves big goals in life. I was only 22 and James was 25. We had no idea of how to care for a baby, let alone two! But we were determined to figure it out, and so we did.

I searched the local bookstores and libraries for information on what to expect when having twins and how to get myself better prepared for the journey ahead. The news spread fast. People we knew – and those we didn't – took the opportunity to share twin birthing stories of 'someone they knew' which left us feeling a tad frightened and disturbed.

We experienced a mixture of emotions, namely joy, fear, excitement and trepidation wrapped up within a bundle of love and respect for each other. James and I would listen to each other's ramblings, processing everything in our minds by seeking out the knowledge we needed and wanted. We then shared what we had learnt with each other – when I let him get a word in that is!

I committed myself to being the best pregnant mum of twins there was!

Had I known then that two years later we would be expecting another set of twins, I may not have been so ambitious.

TWINS AGAIN

Just 17 months after I gave birth to our twin sons, we found out that I was pregnant again. Caleb and Daniel were gorgeous little toddlers who loved to play in the sandpit, smash their cars and trucks into each other and splash each other with bubbles as they threw their toys around in the bath.

Besides their lunch nap, they never stopped moving, and every night when James got home from work, they bounced around the house like excitable lambs, showing him everything they had played with while babbling away with their growing vocabulary.

I remember telling James it felt exactly the same as the first pregnancy, and how I had thought it would feel different being pregnant with just one baby. When I showed him how my pregnant tummy was starting to show at just ten weeks, he casually responded that my tummy was just 'giving way' early after all it had experienced with the boys' pregnancy. Now, although this reasoning was not great for my self-esteem, it was plausible and therefore accepted.

Just getting to our 12-week ultrasound was a mission. I left Caleb and Daniel with some of my playgroup mothers who were having a morning tea at a home nearby. Although they were still so little, they appeared excited about the concept of becoming big brothers and played happily with their little friends.

As we drove to our appointment, we chatted about how the boys might respond to having a baby brother or sister and agreed they would not like sharing mummy and daddy at all. After all, they were the focus of our universe, why change that!

So, when the sonographer once again announced there was a second heartbeat, I think our own hearts skipped a beat! We were literally paralysed, speechless and in shock. I was now 24 years old and James 27, and suddenly we felt ill equipped to process this life-changing news. Feeling stunned and overwhelmed, I asked the sonographer if she was sure. She confirmed that she was positive. 'See, there is Baby One and here is Baby Two,' she said.

After a few seconds of silence, James broke the tension by asking, 'Are there any more in there?'

We laughed nervously, but I knew he was thinking the same thing that I was. While there was great joy, we also knew that a sombre obligation had been placed on our shoulders. There was no bursting champagne corks this time.

We went to a coffee shop after leaving the doctors' office. There was no celebration. Only silence. We stared into our coffee cups as if the barista's decorative swirls were tea leaves telling us our future.

Though our voices were silent, we occasionally looked up at each other. As our eyes met, they spoke volumes, and although our mouths opened, no words came out.

It wasn't that we weren't happy. We were overjoyed. But we knew the addition of not one, but two pairs of pitter-pattering feet meant that our current situation would no longer work. We would need a bigger everything: a bigger house, bigger car and a much bigger budget. We wanted to give these two new babies the best of everything, as we had worked to do for the first two, but didn't know how that would happen.

We could have easily been picked out of a line-up. If the detective walked into the coffee house and said, 'Which of these parents just learned they are having a second set of twins?' anyone could have pointed us out with ease. Once the shock wore off, we set off to do what we had done once before. We encouraged each other by reminding ourselves that we had something of a victory under our belts. After all, our first two were alive and well, despite all of the mishaps, challenges and lack of knowledge from their novice parents. They were 19 months old, into everything and thriving.

By the time we returned to pick up our boys, we had convinced ourselves we would cope. We didn't know how, and we didn't have a choice, but we knew we would be okay. When we told my friends it was twins again, they responded in unison with, 'You must be joking!' It took a few attempts to convince people that our news was true. Caleb and Dan were too young to process the magnitude of the day that catapulted life as we knew it to a whole new stratosphere. When we told them we were now going to have two babies they just smiled and said, 'Yay!'

When word got out about the second twin pregnancy, we didn't receive the joyous celebration of the previous time. Like us, they were stunned.

They started firing questions at us:

- Are you joking?
- How are you going to cope?
- How will you afford them?

We really couldn't blame them. Their reaction was a cocktail of surprise, concern and mind-blowing images of what our new reality would actually look like. You don't get gobsmacked often, but this was one of those moments. We knew they were well intentioned and simply concerned for our welfare, but their responses made us worry even more.

It's amazing how the subconscious mind works at times of stress. One day I had a dream/nightmare that I was having ten babies and James made me line them all up and pick the three I wanted! I woke up so distressed and was actually angry at him for putting me under so much pressure! He just hugged me and said, 'I love you, you crazy woman.'

A few months later, we welcomed Sam and Hannah into the world, and our family was full with three sons and one daughter.

With my first set of twins, I learned a lot from established mothers. I sought them out and wanted to hear all their stories. I was a sponge. I was entering new territory and needed to hear from women who had been there already. That encouraged me to plan appropriately and build a community of support around myself. For the first few months, I went to a mothers' group, and when the babies started to crawl, I moved to a local playgroup and twin club.

But with the second set of twins, 26 months after the first set, I leaned more heavily on my husband and close friends. My husband was a consistent shoulder to rest on, and I needed close family support during this time, more than ever.

Just getting out the door, into the car and arriving at the shops was a massive effort. I'd put Sam and Hannah in a double pram and attach Caleb and Daniel to the sides via reins so they didn't run away. I'd get people asking me if I was a day care mum and when I responded with, 'Do I look like I get to send these kids home at 5pm?' they quietly left me to manage my brood.

If you are thinking, *That's a bit mean, they were just being nice,* I agree. But it appears everyone knows someone with twins, and when they meet a mother with two sets, they feel the need to share their entire life story. By the time I had listened to their jaw-dropping anecdotes, my baby twins were screaming for a feed while my two-year-olds were getting dangerously close to falling into the water fountain. I learnt that when I was on a mission to buy groceries and ended up breastfeeding twins in the middle of a shopping centre, my naturally friendly disposition evaporated. Praise the Lord they now provide nursing mothers with rooms for these moments of desperate need.

I quickly found that, even though I was strong in some areas, there were many parts of me that were vulnerable, defensive and reactive. It's interesting how we don't know how we will respond in certain situations until our limits are tested – and mine were being tested big time.

There is no shame in needing help at this juncture of your life – or any stage of transition, for that matter. The personal and physical load can get heavy at times when you are pregnant and preparing for delivery, especially when you already have toddlers at home. You deserve to be surrounded by a community of support, and when you become honest about how you are travelling, it gives permission for your community to meet you at your place of need.

Never think that you don't have the right kind of strength or the right amount of grit. When you stoically manage this major life change by attempting to project strength you don't genuinely feel, your own needs can easily be overlooked. This is not a test of strength, it's a test of your love.

Just the act of carrying a child is a miracle. A million things need to happen inside a woman's body for this to occur. You deserve to be honoured for that reason alone.

CHAPTER 2

TWINS FACTS

*'Sometimes we are abundantly blessed
without even asking.'*
Annie Gibbins

The mystery of twins is something that astounds parents, doctors, researchers and even twins themselves.

What is this unique and special phenomenon that causes one pregnancy to produce two children?

Why does it happen?

Let's start with the basics!

There are two types of twins:

- Identical or monozygotic.
- Non-identical (fraternal) or dizygotic.

Identical twins develop when one single egg is fertilised by one sperm. Shortly following conception, the embryo splits into two genetically identical babies.

Non-identical twins occur when two separate eggs are released during a monthly ovulation and are fertilised by two different sperm. Both eggs implant and grow independently in the uterus. While one may share similar genetics to the other, they are fraternal, and therefore, not identical.

Firstly, I would heavily suggest you tap into the existing resources and information hubs that provide informed and helpful information regarding twins. Yes, the topic of twins is a phenomenon and without amazing resources, such as Twins Research Australia[1], I wouldn't be the mother of twins that I am today.

- Non-identical twins occur once in approximately every 100 live births.
    - Women can inherit the ability to release multiple eggs during ovulation.
    - Men can carry this gene and pass it on to their daughters.
- Currently, no evidence suggests identical twins are hereditary.
- Women aged 35-40 are three times more likely to give birth to non-identical twins than women aged 20-25.
- Once you have one set of non-identical twins, you are three to four times more likely to have another set.
- Factors including fertility drugs, previous pregnancies and race affect the rate of twins.
    - Nigeria has the highest rate of multiple births and the most identical twins.
    - China has the lowest rate.
- Identical twins are always the same sex.

---

1 twins.org.au

- Fraternal twins are 1/3 male, 1/3 female and 1/3 mixed.
- Zygosity of same-sex twins can be assumed by examining the placentas and fetal membranes post-delivery. However, a DNA test is sometimes required for absolute clarity.
- 40% of twins invent their own languages.
- 70% of babies are born in public hospitals.
- Identical twins have different fingerprints.
- Twins can have completely different skin tones.
- Twins start interacting in the womb at 14 weeks.
- Identical twins can develop different diseases.
- It is possible for fraternal twins to have different fathers.
- Twins can have different birthdays.

Parents can tell the medical community a lot about what it means to raise twins. This anecdotal evidence, combined with a lot of studies, has helped quantify what makes twins similar or distinctly different from every other child in the world.

There are two fun facts about twins that I find particularly interesting. The first is that mothers of twins live longer. Finally, a statistic that benefits me! According to an article in *National Geographic* titled 'Twinning is Winning' covering the work of twin researchers:

> *Robson and Smith used the Utah Population Database, which collects the family trees of people who migrated to Utah in the early 1800s and their descendants. It's one of the most comprehensive sets of family records in the world, and includes data on over 1.6 million people, right up to the 1970s. From these records, the duo pulled out 4,603*

women, all of whom lived in the 19th century, survived till at least the age of 50, and had twins. They compared these women to 54,183 mums of similar characteristics who never had twins.

The duo found that women who gave birth to twins 'outperformed' their peers who only ever had one child at a time. On average, they lived longer after menopause. They gave birth more frequently, and over the course of their lives, they raised two more children. They had children later on into their lives and over a longer part of it. These advantages held even after Robson and Smith adjusted their figures to account for things like the women's age, when they gave birth to their first child, whether their husbands or children died and their religious affiliations.

Ed Yong

Another fun fact that might make you giggle suggests that having twins once can triple or even quadruple your chances of having twins again. This statistic hits home because it is precisely what happened to me. Having two sets of twins, and a fifth child as well, gives me a unique perspective on what it means to be the mother of twins and raise a large family full of constant joys and plenty of surprises.

All new parents have a mammoth task on their hands. Bringing a new life into the world can be taxing on the body, mind, soul, spirit and wallet!

And being a first-time mum is fraught with all sorts of uncertainties. Usually, new mums and dads are younger, inexperienced and worried about how they will fare in this new role. Throw an unstable financial situation into the mix and you can see why having a baby is a monumental task in any person's life and the life of their partner.

When you double the number of babies in the womb, you exponentially increase the level of difficulty. There are special considerations twin mums need to face that other new parents never even think of. But there is also a whole range of joys and amazements that make up for any of the challenges ten times over.

I love telling the stories of our family's journey, especially now that my children are all adults, and there is no better story than the story of a child's birth. Each is a uniquely different experience. In fact, I don't think I have ever heard two birth stories that were exactly the same. There is always something special, or heart-wrenching, or miraculous in every woman's life-giving story. I have committed myself to supporting mothers of twins by sharing my story, hearing their stories and helping to educate and inspire in any way that I can.

In the coming pages, I will share my journey as a mum of two sets of twins. I will also share some of the best practices that exist today. As you dive into this book, know there is a community of people that stretches around the world, who are there to support you and cheer you on.

CHAPTER 3

THE PREGNANCY JOURNEY BEGINS

'Whether your pregnancy was meticulously planned or a complete surprise, one thing is for certain: twice the smiles and twice the love are heading your way.'
Annie Gibbins

In Chapter 1, I shared my experience of how my husband and I discovered we were expecting twins twice. It was all so jaw dropping, and I just couldn't wait a moment longer to share those special moments with you. However, it's important that you know what happened before and after the big 'twins reveal', to give you a clearer picture of what lies ahead.

Firstly, if you have completed a home pregnancy kit and you have seen the big news that your test reads positive, congratulations!

TWINS

WHEN SHOULD MY FIRST PRENATAL VISIT TAKE PLACE?

Typically, your first prenatal visit will occur in the second month of pregnancy and is usually with your local general practitioner who will confirm your pregnancy and refer you to the local hospital or private obstetrician for future appointments.

When I was six weeks pregnant, before I knew I was expecting twins, I made an appointment to see my local doctor, and me being me, I arrived with an extensive list of questions.

- Can you confirm that I'm pregnant?
- When is my due date?
- What is the best way to manage morning sickness?
- How long does morning sickness last?
- What can I take to reduce its severity?
- What changes should I make to my diet?
- Will I have cravings?
- What foods and beverages should I avoid during pregnancy?
- How much weight should I expect to gain during my pregnancy?
- How much should I be exercising?
- What types of exercise should I avoid?
- Is sex still okay and for how long?
- How does pregnancy impact work and travel requirements?
- Can I continue taking my current medications?
- Who will manage my care during my pregnancy?

Before I had a chance to work through my list of questions,

he suggested we start with a urine test and sent me off to the bathroom to urinate on a pregnancy stick. As he watched, the test confirmed my pregnancy; he smiled and then congratulated me on this exciting moment.

Armed with his own checklist (I love a list), he collected my full medical history to build a better picture of what was to come. If you are in the early stages of pregnancy, these are some examples of what you could be asked:

General medical history: You will likely be asked about any immunisations, major illnesses, surgeries, known allergies, drugs, medications and supplements, including herbs and vitamins.

Mental health history: Be honest with any former or current mental health challenges including anxiety, depression and any other conditions.

Obstetric profile: It is extremely important to detail any previous pregnancies, including complications or losses, and details about previous deliveries.

Gynaecological background: Your early adult health profile will offer insight, from the age of your first period, menstruation cycle, occurrences of premenstrual syndrome (PMS), prior gynaecological surgeries, abnormal Pap smears or any contracted sexually transmitted infections (STI).

Disease exposure: If you have contracted or been exposed to any contagious diseases, this information can be vital, should any future abnormalities occur.

Family medical history: Conditions such as diabetes, cancer, kidney disease, epilepsy or high blood pressure are a sample of hereditary health conditions to be checked by both parents.

After finishing his suite of questions and urine test for the human chorionic gonadotropin (HCG) hormone, he recommended my list of questions would best be answered by my obstetrician at my first prenatal appointment and wrote me a referral. My time was up, and I was shown the door.

So, after this mini appointment, a few phone calls to experienced mothers and a trip to the local library, I could tick off the following points:

Q. Can you confirm that I'm pregnant?
A. Yes.

Q. When is my due date?
A. Initially estimated from the date of my last menstruation, my due date was pinned for 20 April 1991. Please note, this date may change after your ultrasound.

Q. What causes morning sickness?
A. Mild morning sickness doesn't harm you or your baby and is thought to be caused by low blood sugar or increased pregnancy hormones.

Q. What is the best way to manage morning sickness?
A. Avoid large meals and eat small, regular snacks, avoiding foods and smells that trigger nausea. Sip water regularly, try to breathe in fresh clean air and stay relaxed.

Q. How long does morning sickness last?
A. At least seven in ten pregnant women have morning sickness in the first trimester (first three months) of pregnancy. It usually starts at approximately six weeks into pregnancy and will peak at week nine. For some of us it lasts all day long! Most women feel significantly better in their second trimester, but some have morning sickness throughout pregnancy.

Q. What if I can't stop vomiting or if it makes me dizzy?
A. Approximately 3% of women experience excessive nausea and vomiting during pregnancy and are prone to feeling dizzy, fainting, losing weight and can become dehydrated (hyperemesis gravidarum). These women need medical treatment to help keep them and their baby safe. If you experience any doubt, I urge you to visit your health care professional. Don't be brave or stoic.

Q. What changes should I make to my diet?
A. Throughout your pregnancy, try to consume a wide variety of foods, including lean meats, whole grains, fruits, vegetables and unsaturated fats. The Australian Dietary Guidelines[1] recommends daily servings for pregnant women from at least five food groups. Your need for certain nutrients (such as iron, iodine and folate) increases when you are pregnant, so you may need to take

---

1 eatforhealth.gov.au

supplements, for example folate and vitamin D. Your blood tests will identify your body's specific requirements, so utilise all the information you have regarding your medical make-up.

A standard pregnancy diet recommends:

- A variety of fruits and vegetables of different types and colours. Ideally two serves of fruit and five serves of vegetables every day.
- An increase of wholegrains and high-fibre foods.
- Iron-rich foods such as lean red meat or tofu.
- Calcium-enriched foods such as milk, hard cheese and yoghurt.
- Drinking plenty of water.

Q. Will I have cravings?
A. Maybe. It is thought food cravings and sudden food aversions may have something to with the effects of pregnancy hormones, which can alter the way some foods taste and smell. You may have a craving for foods you already love (big win here) or certain foods you've never laid your eyes on. For example, my body must have been craving salt as I felt a strong desire to eat Twisties. It is okay to give in to the occasional food craving, as long as you continue to eat a good variety of healthy foods. It's all about balance.

Q. What foods and beverages should I avoid during pregnancy?
A. Where possible, limit your intake of foods and drinks high in saturated fat, added sugar and salt, and say goodbye to alcohol!

Q. How much weight should I expect to gain during my pregnancy?
A. This can vary woman to woman and can depend on your current body mass index (BMI) measurement. Typically, most women will gain between 25-30lbs in weight during pregnancy.

Q. When do I schedule my ultrasounds?
A. Prenatal ultrasounds are routinely scheduled at 12-13 weeks, 20 weeks and then as required up to the birth. Typically, your assigned medical professional and practice will guide the regularity of your scans, however it is important to note these may differ depending on your pregnancy state.

Q. How much should I be exercising?
A. Throughout the trimesters, the body's needs will expectedly shift, and an exercise regime should be as adaptable as the pregnancy! For most pregnant women, at least 30 minutes of moderate-intensity exercise is recommended on most, if not all, days of the week. Walking is a great exercise for beginners. It provides moderate aerobic conditioning with minimal stress on your joints. I would always recommend seeking out trainers or fitness centres that specialise in prenatal exercise regimes.

Q. What types of exercise should I avoid?
A. Your body will likely guide what you can and cannot do. However, do not lie flat on your back for long periods, particularly after 16 weeks, because the weight of your bump presses on the main blood vessel bringing blood back to your heart and this

can make you faint. Avoid contact sports and any high-intensity activities that place pressure or compression to the heart.

Q. Is sex still okay and for how long?
A. The good news is, yes. Sex is a natural, normal part of pregnancy – if you're having a normal pregnancy. Penetration and intercourse's movement won't harm the baby, who is protected by your abdomen and the uterus' muscular walls. Your baby is also cushioned by the amniotic sac's fluid. If, for any medical reason, your medical professional advises you against sex, please listen to their advice.

Q. How does pregnancy impact work and travel requirements?
A. Throughout your pregnancy, your body will experience a multitude of changes, such as increased tiredness, nausea and lower energy levels. If your job requires you to travel, it is important to ensure you take extra rest breaks. Should your work require air travel, then please follow the safety guidelines and recommendations from your travel provider. Some women will work to their due date, others will choose to take maternity leave prior to the birth to prepare for the arrival of a newborn. Do what is right for you and always consult your employer regarding maternity allowances.

Q. Can I continue taking my current medications?
A. As I am not a qualified doctor, this is not one for me. Please consult your medical professional on medication guidelines during your pregnancy.

Q. Who will manage my care during my pregnancy?
A. I was asked if I had a preference in seeing a private or public obstetrician and was then provided a referral to make an appointment. We found the choice highly personal, and our decision came down to a number of factors which were important to us. Research, absorb and ask all the right questions when determining your care providers during pregnancy[1].

A new Q&A list evolved as I needed to book my first prenatal care appointment and I needed to know where it would be.

PUBLIC VERSUS PRIVATE

In Australia, patients can often choose whether they want to be cared for in a public or a private hospital. Your choice of hospital will depend on your personal circumstances, where you live, whether you want to choose your own doctor, your budget and whether you have private health insurance cover. Approximately 70% of babies are born in a public hospital where there is a lower chance of having an intervention, such as a caesarean.

Australia's public hospitals provide high-quality medical care and are free of charge. All pregnancy consultations, delivery, hospital stays and even some postnatal care are fully covered by Medicare. However, some services performed outside of a hospital setting, including ultrasounds, are not.

You will typically be cared for by the midwives who are on shift at the time of your prenatal appointments and delivery. After giving birth, you will share a public room with one or more

---
1 healthdirect.gov.au/understanding-the-public-and-private-hospital-systems

new mothers and your time in hospital will be determined by your medical needs.

In the private system, you get to choose your obstetrician. If, like me, you don't know who to ask for, this choice may be based on recommendations made by family, friends or simply who works at your preferred private hospital.

Please be aware your private obstetrician may prefer that your twins are born in a public hospital if they feel it is better equipped for your complex needs. As private health insurance cannot cover out-of-hospital medical services, including consultations with specialists in their own clinics and rooms, the majority of your bill will come from your obstetrician's fees.

Your chosen obstetrician will be the one who provides your professional care at all pregnancy appointments and the birth itself. If for some reason they become unavailable, they will send a colleague to act in their place. You will also get your own room, sometimes with a double bed, and will typically stay for four to five days.

Considering I didn't know what many of my needs would be, I found this decision huge.

BUDGET

In a recent study, Griffith University research found women who gave birth in the public system paid, on average, $500 in out-of-pocket costs from conception through to 12 months postpartum, whereas private costs were approximately $3,000. Personal items including sanitary products, toiletries, breast pads and nipple cream are your own responsibility.

INSURANCE

If you have invested in private insurance, you will need to check your policy to see if pregnancy cover is included. It's often one of those optional extras, and pregnancy cover typically includes a 12-month wait time for a new or upgraded policy. There is no easy solution if you do not plan ahead. Rebates will also differ depending on the coverage provided by your health fund.

CHAPTER 4

LIFE DURING PREGNANCY

'Trust your pregnant body to know its innate power and strength.'
Annie Gibbins

We are very fortunate in Australia to have high-quality care offered in our public and private hospitals; however, we chose private as I had health insurance and wanted to see the same obstetrician throughout my pregnancy. You will need to thoroughly research what is provided in your geographical area as standards of care vary significantly around the world.

My first obstetric visit was very comprehensive, and massively extended on the information provided in the referral documentation.

As you read earlier on in the book, the ultrasound revealed that we were expecting twins, and it didn't take long for the obstetrician to phone me offering his congratulations. He also took this opportunity to bring forward my next appointment.

Once you find out that you are having twins, prepare for your obstetrician or midwife to be very cautious. You may find that you are being monitored more often than with other pregnancies, and this is completely normal.

If it's your first pregnancy, you'll never know the difference! Double the baby count in utero means twice the possibility of complex issues, so your doctor or midwife will want to keep a close eye on your health (and your babies') to minimise the risk. It literally takes extra time to chase both babies around your womb to check, measure and record essential medical information, so expect long appointments.

FIRST TRIMESTER

In the first trimester, you may experience the following common symptoms, and it would be beneficial to plan your life around them:

- Nausea.
- Vomiting.
- Swollen or sensitive breasts.
- Areola (skin on your nipples) darkening.
- Bloating.
- Food cravings.
- Sensitivity to smells.
- Exhaustion.
- Urinary tract infections.
- Heartburn.
- Oily skin.

- Hair and nails growing faster.
- Bluish tint on your vulva.
- Feeling moody.
- Constipation.
- Needing to urinate more often.
- Skin on and around cheeks, nose and eyes darkening.
- Starting to gain weight.

While externally I looked the same, my invisible transformation had started with a punch. Early hormonal changes meant my breasts started to swell and became more sensitive, I urinated more often and morning sickness lasted most of the day. Emotionally I felt excited, anxious and exhausted – often all in one day.

While I didn't suffer too much fatigue, I was surprised by how fast the nausea hit. To reduce the time with my head in the toilet, I avoided my known odour triggers and experimented with eating small, frequent meals. Taking citrus fruits, chocolate, spice and fried foods off the menu seemed to help reduce my nausea and heartburn.

After hearing high levels of progesterone can cause constipation, I kept up my physical exercise, high-fibre diet and fluids as best I could. I made sure to engage in a walk or swim most days, but sometimes light exercises from the sofa was the best I could do.

When I compared my experience with other pregnant friends, it amazed me how different our physical responses were in those early weeks.

NUTRITION AROUND MORNING SICKNESS

It goes without saying that good nutrition is critical for the healthy development of your babies, so get into some fresh food cooking with seasonal fruits and vegetables. Healthy food pyramid diagrams and guidelines are always helpful to revisit.

To avoid the overwhelm around what foods you should consume more or less of, I found it helpful to follow the recommendations of published nutritionists.

WHAT'S OKAY AND WHAT'S NOT!

If you find it hard to give up your guilty pleasures, you are not alone. But this will only be for nine months, and I assure you, it will be worth it – so give it a red-hot go! While some changes can be modified over days or weeks, alcohol, cigarettes and other drugs should be stopped immediately.

For specific medical advice, please consult with your health care provider.

You should also be aware of two important concepts: the placental barrier and the breastmilk barrier. Your babies are protected by the placenta which serves as a barrier to keep out harmful elements. Your breastmilk also has a natural barrier that helps protect the breastmilk supply.

Some foods, drugs, lifestyle choices and herbs are unable to be absorbed through these barriers and your babies' breastmilk will be protected. You should avoid anything that might harm your babies or spoil your breastmilk. For example:

ALCOHOL AND BABIES DON'T MIX

One of the primary concerns with alcohol consumption is that it increases the risk of a low birth weight. And since twins are typically at high risk of low birth weight, this makes the choice to abstain even more important.

According to many of the world's respected health care organisations, such as the Centers for Disease Control (CDC), doctors recommend abstaining from alcohol altogether as it can be absorbed by the placental barrier, and in the first trimester, can affect unborn babies' brain and facial features.

Once your babies are born, alcohol enters the breastmilk, so if you intend on having a tipple or two, you will need to substitute your babies' feed with previously expressed milk or give them formula for the following two days. It also requires expressing with a breast pump and throwing out the milk produced during those two days – so for me, that all felt like too much effort for a glass or two of bubbly.

WHEN COFFEE IS NO LONGER YOUR GO-TO

The American College of Obstetricians and Gynaecologists (ACOG) recommend eliminating, or at least drastically reducing, intake of any caffeinated beverages. Like alcohol, caffeine crosses over the placental barrier with no trouble at all and can reduce your babies' birth weight. So, if you are one of the many people who struggle to start your day without a cup of coffee, you will need to explore new beverage choices. The daily recommended quantity is 200 micrograms (mcg) of caffeine, and that's not going to 'cut it' for diehard coffee lovers. Now could be the perfect time to try iced tea with lunch or immerse yourself in pure natural H_2O.

CHOOSE YOUR FISH CAREFULLY

While fish can be good for you and your babies due to the high levels of omega-3s, certain fish products are also high in mercury, which can affect your babies' central nervous system. Some varieties of fish you might consider avoiding are:

- Marlin.
- Tuna (especially bigeye tuna).
- Roughy (especially orange roughy).
- Shark.
- Tilefish.
- Swordfish.
- Raw fish of any kind.

RAW MEAT, RAW EGGS, UNDERCOOKED MEAT, ORGAN MEAT AND PROCESSED MEAT

Raw and undercooked meat provide a happy home for all kinds of bacteria and pathogens that are harmful during pregnancy. You may enjoy a rare steak, but it's best to wait until after the babies are born to consume it. Raw eggs can hide in foods where you do not normally expect them to linger, such as icing, homemade mayo and hollandaise sauce, eggs over easy, homemade salad dressing and homemade ice cream.

Most professionals recommend against organ meat, such as liver and kidneys, as they have been linked to miscarriage and congenital malformations.

RAW SPROUTS AND UNWASHED PRODUCE

I know, this is quite a list. But trust me. Seeing your babies' happy faces will be well worth the wait. Due to the risk of salmonella, listeria and parasites, you should avoid raw sprouts, although cooked sprouts are fine.

VITAMINS

Some studies suggest that 400mcg of folic acid in the first trimester can reduce the likelihood of certain birth defects. Your midwife or doctor may prescribe a prenatal vitamin that is packed with nutrients for you and your baby such as:

- Vitamin D.
- Folic acid.
- Vitamin C.
- Calcium.
- Riboflavin.
- Zinc.
- Iron.
- Iodine.
- Vitamin B12.
- Thiamine.
- Choline.

EXERCISE

Besides being good for your weight and circulation, I found staying active helped to improve my posture and decreased backaches, ankle swelling and fatigue. I also love the way it works to minimise gestational diabetes, reduce stress and equip you with the stamina required for healthy childbirth. While it can be a challenge to get moving every day, once your babies are born, you will be thankful that you increased your strength and stamina as you will be busy carrying, pushing and then chasing one or more little crawlers around the house.

If you have any of the following symptoms, please consult your medical practitioner prior to increasing your activity:

- Bleeding or spotting.
- Low placenta.
- Threatened or recurrent miscarriage.
- Previous premature births or history of early labour.
- Weak cervix.

If you are used to engaging in more physical activities, start reducing the impact and intensity in your training.

CLOTHING

While most women can wear regular clothes for most of the first trimester, some may start sizing up a little earlier. In addition to getting some loose-fitting garments, you will also soon need a larger bra. By four to five months, most of your clothes won't fit, so shop around for a new look that will work for you. I loved being swaddled in cotton as I felt comfortable in the fabric's breathability and softness. I also wore leggings with loose-fitting tops and cardigans or blazers. I kept my heels low and played around with different fabrics and prints which complimented my changing shape and showed off my bump.

TWINS

SECOND TRIMESTER

Your body will undergo some major changes during the second trimester, and you will hopefully find the sweet spot where you feel fabulous and look glowing, most of the time. I remember being so excited when I felt the babies move for the first time and laughed when their bouts of hiccups felt like a table tennis match inside my abdomen.

I used this time to read baby books, plan the nursery, book into prenatal classes, see the dentist, improve my diet, modify my exercise, attend scheduled prenatal care appointments, take my prenatal vitamins, sleep more, rest more, and play with and talk to my growing bump.

As my breasts and abdomen grew and felt itchy from the stretching, I rubbed them with anti-stretch-mark cream to keep moisture in their upper layers and improve the skin's elasticity. It was a beautiful time watching my body blossom and grow in such a magical way.

If you are like me and have heard the news from your ultrasound that you are now pregnant with twins, please take the time to enjoy every moment of weeks 13-27, as they are a gift that will set you up beautifully for your final trimester.

While most mums have healthy twin pregnancies, you and your babies will need extra care because pregnancies with multiples can be more complicated than singleton pregnancies. Whilst we don't need to be alarmed, we do need to be aware of the risks and be mindful of them.

For example, women expecting twins are two to five times more likely to develop high blood pressure or pre-eclampsia and need to be monitored closely to reduce the chance of placental abruption (early detachment of the placenta).

If you wish to read up on all potential risks, there are highly credible websites and textbooks to provide you with information on topics like birth defects, vanishing twin syndrome, twin-to-twin transfusion syndrome and amniotic fluid irregularities. My advice is not to burden yourself with the hypothetical what-ifs and instead focus on the here and now. Attend all of your appointments. Get the recommended tests done. Be proactive in all aspects of your health and wellness, so, if a challenge does arise, you have more time and energy to deal with it.

WHEN THINGS DON'T GO AS PLANNED

As you get closer to the end of the second trimester, you may find that your doctor or midwife wants to see you more often. This is designed to measure the babies' heart rates, fetal growth and movement.

Pregnancy tracker apps are great for storing day-to-day information, like baby movements.

If your doctor has any concerns, additional tests may be ordered. Your doctor's primary goal is to keep the babies safely in utero for as long as possible. Preterm labour is one of the major problems mothers of twins may experience, so if you do begin contractions prematurely, your doctor may order bed rest.

BED REST IS NOT AS EASY AS IT SOUNDS

Some pretty strange things can happen when you are pregnant with twins. Everything from early contractions, low fetal movement and haemorrhaging can cause new mums to panic and assume the worst. But you are blessed to be having children in an era where medical knowledge is advancing rapidly and technology is nothing short of astounding.

Still, there is one remedy for mums experiencing issues during pregnancy that no machine can duplicate, and that's bed rest. It is one of the most common recommendations for mums of twins and perhaps one of the most dreaded.

When non-pregnant people hear about bed rest, they chuckle and make a flippant comment about how they would love to be ordered to bed. They somehow imagine themselves being fanned by Egyptian maidens and fed grapes by hunky men while they watch re-runs of their favourite Netflix shows for hours and hours.

They imagine it to be nothing more than leisure, and they are right … for the first 15 minutes.

It's funny that people always claim they want rest until it's prescribed by a doctor. As the age-old saying goes, 'Be careful what you wish for.'

As soon as the doctor says stay off your feet, your mind begins to ticker tape the 900 things you have to do. Suddenly, the nursery must be painted, the closets must be organised and the kitchen must be cleaned to within an inch of its life.

You couldn't stay still if someone handcuffed you to the bed. And if you already have other children, it requires high-level managerial skills.

Bed rest is a common treatment for preterm labour and other issues with twin mums because gravity is not a friend to the woman carrying two babies at one time. The pressure on the uterus is strong and can send you into labour before your babies are ready to be born.

Bed rest could be prescribed for any length of time. Usually, it is just a few days up to a couple of weeks. But your doctor may be concerned enough to suggest that you remain on bed rest for the remainder of your pregnancy.

That can be hard to hear when you are still in your second trimester. But as beneficial as bed rest is, it is hard to stay off your feet and lie in bed all day. You can only watch so much TV, read so many books and fill in so many crossword puzzles before you feel that you are going to go stir-crazy.

Try these solutions to improve your time off your feet:

KEEP YOUR BABIES IN MIND
Babies develop at a rapid rate. In fact, if you think about it, it is quite unbelievable that a woman can grow an entire human in less than a year! So, a lot can happen in as little as a week.

The point is that every extra day you can give your babies in your womb improves their chances for a problem-free birth.

REST IN DIFFERENT PLACES
Staying off your feet doesn't have to be done only in bed. You can sit in a reclining chair or stretch out on the couch. Going outside and laying down on patio furniture gives you the added benefits of sunshine and fresh air.

TRY ELEVATING YOUR FEET
If your belly allows, laying down will feel better if you can raise your feet a bit. That will keep the fluids from gathering in your feet and making them feel bloated, tight and swollen.

VARIETY IS KEY

Consider all of the things you can now do that you never had time to do in the past. Set a goal for yourself to reach a certain level on your language learning app. Practise singing. You've been given the gift of time!

Read the classics. Take an online course. Take up macramé, knitting, crocheting or cross-stitching. With a lap table and a little caution, you can do almost anything. Use bed rest to connect with your spouse emotionally and physically. Without getting graphic, bed rest can be shared with your spouse as time for bonding.

Watch a movie together, cuddle, listen to music or read a romance novel to each other. If you and your partner have iPhones and like games, consider downloading GamePigeon. It allows you to sit side by side (or anywhere, really) and play all kinds of fun games together. It can really help to pass the time.

CONSIDER TAKING TIME OFF FROM WORK

Remember, you are not just resting your body, you should also rest your heart, mind, soul and spirit. So, if you have a particularly stressful job, it might mean you need to go on leave earlier than expected.

GET YOUR KIDS IN ON THE ACT

If you have children at home, you will have special challenges. Toddlers still need to be cared for while you are supposed to be resting. Some parents have the toddler play on the bed and only get up to feed them, but if you have an especially active toddler, it might be time to call in the cavalry.

If you can find friends or family who can entertain your little ones, let them help you for a few weeks. You may even make use of day care.

THIRD TRIMESTER

There is so much happening in the final trimester, and it's so important that you slow down the tempo and focus on keeping yourself rested, comfortable and prepared for the safe delivery of your twins. As their size and weight increases, so does the toll on your body, which is huge, and you need to be extremely kind to yourself.

According to John Hopkins:

- Blood pressure may decrease as the babies press on the main vein that returns blood to the heart.
- Swelling of the ankles, hands and face may happen (called oedema) as you continue to retain fluids.
- Hair may begin to grow on your arms, legs and face due to increased hormone stimulation of hair follicles. Hair may also feel coarser.
- Leg cramps may happen more often.
- Braxton Hicks contractions (false labour) may begin to happen at irregular intervals in preparation for childbirth.
- Stretch marks may appear on the stomach, breast, thighs and buttocks.
- Colostrum (a fluid in the breasts that nourishes the baby until the breastmilk becomes available) may begin to leak from your nipples.

- Dry, itchy skin may persist, particularly on the stomach, as the skin continues to grow and stretch.
- Your libido (sex drive) may decrease.
- Skin pigmentation may become more apparent, especially dark patches of skin on the face.
- Constipation, heartburn and indigestion may continue.
- You will have increased white-coloured vaginal discharge (leucorrhoea), which may contain more mucus.
- Backaches may persist and increase in intensity.
- Haemorrhoids may persist and increase in severity.
- Varicose veins in the legs may persist and increase in severity.[1]

Besides feeling fabulous for most of the second trimester, from 30 weeks gestation I experienced an unusual condition called intrahepatic cholestasis. This diagnosis is a liver condition caused by a slowing of the normal flow of bile. As my liver struggled to produce the digestive fluid it needed to break down fats, my bile salts built up and entered my bloodstream. This resulted in intense itching, all day every day, which made me look like a pregnant ice addict, as there was no rash to explain why I was scratching the skin off my arms. Sadly, with this condition, the recurrence rate is 60-90%, so during my second twin pregnancy I fortunately knew what was happening.

Once I heard my symptoms would disappear as soon as the twins were born, I was desperate to get my babies out as early as possible, and besides shedding regular tears, was told they weren't physically ready to come into the world until 36 weeks.

---
1 hopkinsmedicine.org/health/wellness-and-prevention/the-third-trimester

Patience was not my friend. However, their health was so much more important to me.

As my size exploded, I got more comfortable with not being able to see my toes and having to sit down to put on shoes. James used to laugh when I could rest my dinner plate flat across the top of my abdomen! I seriously felt like I was going to be the size of a house forever.

I'd lie awake at night arching my back to expand my abdominal cavity just so I could take a few big breaths in as the babies stretched, kicked and consumed all available space. Their tiny body parts protruded as they got comfortable in a new position, and I seriously felt like I might burst if I got any bigger. I won't lie, I was also thinking about how on earth they were going to get out of me! I did everything to put those thoughts out of my mind as it just didn't feel pleasant!

By the final weeks, it was easier to get out of bed, have a quick wee and then slide back in rather than turn my massive abdomen over in one sweeping move. Plus, the pressure being placed on my bladder meant urinary frequency had gone to a whole new level.

Your prenatal care specialist will be is closely monitoring your babies':

- Weight.
- Blood pressure.
- Urine.
- Position.
- Growth.
- Development.

- Fundal height.
- Heartbeats.

Those last few weeks were tough, especially in the heat of an Australian summer with local bushfires, but the day did come when I could say goodbye to incessant scratching, my gigantic abdomen and frequent mini 'wees' and get ready to say hello to these two gorgeous little humans.

For Standard Pregnancy Appointment schedule, see Appendix 1

CHAPTER 5

PREPARING FOR BIRTH

'Preparing to give life provides a rare opportunity to intertwine the mind, body and spirit of two lovers, basking in the joy of their creation.'
Annie Gibbins

We all have our own twin pregnancy journey – some easier, some harder. But ultimately, we aim for that moment when the time is right for those little ones to come into this world. We want to meet them with a safe, secure and well-equipped environment, and be prepared to nurture them every step of the way.

You will get lots of birthing advice from people who have never delivered twins and will quickly learn to say thank you and move on. There are plenty of mums, like me, who are more than happy to share what it's like to give birth to twins, but remember, we had our experience and you will have yours. Mothers will tell you how our bodies were able to rise to the task of bringing our babies into the world and you will be less daunted by the concerns of those who wonder how you will pull off such a mammoth task.

WHAT IF …

Allow me to inoculate you against a social virus that will inevitably attack. It comes in the form of seemingly endless what-if questions from people in your social circle. They may want to give input on your birthing decisions or discourage some of the choices you make. I learned early on that I had to guard against the effects of the what-ifs. People will project their fears on you – solicited or unsolicited. Remain strong about your birthing decisions while remaining open to learn from people who have something of value and expertise to share.

ONE IMPORTANT CAVEAT
If the what-ifs are coming from your partner, you should view them completely differently from the random musings of outsiders. Your partner, quite literally, has skin in the game. These are their babies too, and you are the person they are committed to. Your partner's questions will be coming from a completely different motivation. Take those questions seriously and provide them with all of the information that helped you to make your decision. It's important you have a vision together of what you want your twins' birth experience to be.

Remember that your partner's energy is inside you. You shared in the creation of new life, so it's important to honour their concerns and do your best to address them. They are your ally. Address their questions kindly. Ask for their support by explaining how important it is to you. Ask what parameters and safeguards you can put in place to give them a greater sense of comfort.

Also, remember that you are the captain of this ship. Birthing decisions are made with your partner, your inner circle and your medical team. You may have to consider setting boundaries that are firm and clear when it comes to others who want to countermand your choices. Usually, a loving comment that you would appreciate their support is all that is needed. This helps to protect your sanity!

While apprehension can feel real and valid, knowledge conquers fear. Now is your time to focus on your impending birth.

WHAT THE EXPERTS SAY TO EXPECT

During the late stages of your pregnancy, your health care team will carry out regular health checks of you and your babies. These checks will strongly influence your delivery. If you are less than 37 weeks pregnant and you experience any of the signs of premature labour, such as contractions, your water breaking, bleeding, a 'show' of mucus from your vagina or a sudden decrease in your babies' movements, contact your doctor or nearest delivery suite immediately. It may be possible to slow down or stop the labour to improve their optimal health on delivery.

As you prepare your birth plan, be thinking about how you can connect with your babies, and how your partner can too, as soon after their birth as possible.

Ask yourself:

- What do my partner and I want?
- What do my partner and I need?
- What do my babies need?

- Am I ready to trust myself and trust my body to do what it is wired to do?
- What do I want my babies' first moments on this side of the womb to be like?
- What do I want them to see, hear, smell, feel and touch in those important first seconds of life?
- What medical interventions and tests am I comfortable with?
- If my babies are healthy, do I want to hold them immediately?
- How soon do I want to begin breastfeeding?

Imagine what the birth could be like and keep your mind open to the many alternate situations that may eventuate, such as:

- Having your babies placed on your chest soon after delivery.
- Delaying weighing and measuring to allow time for skin-to-skin contact.
- Breastfeeding your babies immediately after birth.
- Having your partner make skin-to-skin contact with both of the babies after you are done with the first breastfeed.

EXPECT TO DELIVER EARLY

In Australia, approximately one in every ten babies are born prematurely with more than 60% of twins born before 37 weeks. While most are born between 32 and 36 weeks and don't have any serious long-term problems, every day counts in utero.

Most babies born before 32 weeks, and those weighing 2.5kg or less, may need help breathing and may be cared for in a neonatal intensive care unit (NICU) until they have developed enough to survive on their own. Babies born between 32 and 37 weeks may need care in a special care nursery (SCN).

Additionally, premature babies have lower birth weights and may need help breathing, eating, fighting infection and staying warm. Very premature babies, those born before 28 weeks, are especially vulnerable.

For this reason, one or both babies may need care in a neonatal intensive care unit (NICU) as they need specialised medical support immediately post-delivery, so be generous when packing your hospital bag.

NATURAL CHILDBIRTH

It is best for very premature babies to be born at a hospital that has an NICU. If the hospital where the babies are born does not have an NICU, you may be transferred to another hospital.

When you are in labour, you may be given medicines to stop the contractions for a while. This allows you to be transferred to another hospital if necessary. You may also receive injections of corticosteroids 12-24 hours before the birth to help your babies' lungs function more efficiently.

Premature babies can be born very quickly and will usually be born through the vagina. However, in some cases the doctor may decide it is safest to deliver the baby via caesarean. Your doctor will discuss this decision with you.

A medical team from the neonatal (newborn) unit will be there for the birth. As soon as your babies are born, they will care for them in your birthing suite, possibly using a neonatal resuscitation bed. The team will keep your babies warm and help them to breathe with an oxygen mask or breathing tube, and possibly administer other medicines.

Once your babies are stable, they may be transferred to the NICU or SCN.

CAESAREAN

Approximately one in three babies in Australia are born by caesarean. This is higher than the rate in many other developed countries and still more likely in the private sector.

A caesarean might be planned if you develop pregnancy complications. But sometimes the need for a caesarean does not become clear until labour is underway. In an emergency, the babies may need to be delivered very quickly.

A caesarean section is a surgical procedure to deliver a baby through a cut in the mother's abdomen and uterus. There are several medical reasons why you might plan for a caesarean, or your medical team might decide it's safest for you to have an emergency caesarean after labour begins. If this wasn't considered as part of your birthing plan, the shock can be quite overwhelming. But remember, the health of you and your babies comes first.

WHY MIGHT YOU NEED A CAESAREAN?

The most common reasons for needing a caesarean are:

- You are pregnant with twins and one or both are in the breech position (bottom first).

- One of your babies is transverse (sideways) and can't be manually turned.
- Your placenta is partly or completely covering the cervix.
- You have had a previous caesarean.

WHAT HAPPENS DURING THE OPERATION?

Firstly, you will usually receive a regional anaesthetic, such as an epidural, which numbs the lower part of your body. This means you will get to be awake throughout the operation. Sometimes emergency caesareans must be done under general anaesthetic, which means you won't be conscious during the birth.

Your tummy will be cleaned and a tube, known as a catheter, will be inserted into your bladder to collect urine.

The obstetrician will make a cut through the wall of your tummy, usually low and across near the pubic hair line. If your babies need to be delivered very quickly, the cut may be made vertically from just below the belly button to above the pubic bone. The doctor will then cut through the layers of fatty tissue and muscle, and finally cut through the uterus.

The babies are delivered through the cuts. The doctor will clear the babies' noses and mouths of fluids and clamp the umbilical cords. If you are awake, they will hold your babies up so that you can see. This is a joyous moment. They will then remove the placenta and close the cuts with stitches or staples.

If you are awake, you will feel tugging and pulling, but not pain, and you will also hear fluid being suctioned. A screen will be put across your chest so you cannot see what is happening. It can be very surreal, but motherhood often is, so embrace how your babies enter the world, in whatever form that takes.

The operation takes approximately 30-40 minutes, with the babies usually born in the first ten minutes. If you are awake, you will be able to see your babies immediately.

WHO WILL BE IN THE ROOM?

Your partner or support person will usually be able to be with you during the caesarean. There may also be a lot of medical staff, including:

- Obstetrician – performs the operation and delivers the babies.
- Anaesthetist – administers the anaesthetic.
- Scrub nurse – passes instruments to the obstetrician.
- Scout nurse – assists the scrub nurse.
- Anaesthetic nurse – assists the anaesthetist.
- Paediatrician – looks after the babies after the birth.
- Midwife – receives the babies once born and looks after them until you return to the ward.
- Theatre technician – looks after the operating theatre and helps you on and off the table.

PAIN RELIEF OPTIONS

The types of anaesthetic used in caesareans differ. Your doctor will choose the most appropriate for you.

EPIDURAL

When you get an epidural, you receive a local anaesthetic, then a hollow needle and a small, flexible catheter are inserted near the spinal cord in your back. The needle is removed, leaving the catheter in place. Anaesthetic medicine is injected through the catheter and can be topped up later.

SPINAL BLOCK

A spinal block injects a single dose of anaesthetic directly into the cerebrospinal fluid around the spinal cord. You will go numb very quickly, but the amount of anaesthetic cannot be topped up.

GENERAL ANAESTHETIC

You might be given a general anaesthetic if the regional anaesthetic doesn't work, there isn't time for a regional anaesthetic or the babies' lives are threatened.

RISKS AND COMPLICATIONS

Caesareans are safe, however, like all major surgeries, there are risks to you, which include:

- Blood loss.
- Blood clots.
- Infection in the wound.
- Problems with the anaesthetic.
- Possible damage to other organs nearby, such as the bladder.

Recovery from a caesarean takes longer than recovery from a vaginal birth. If you have a caesarean, your future pregnancies will be considered higher risk, and there are also more risks with future caesareans.

Sometimes babies born by caesarean can have temporary trouble breathing. The midwife and paediatrician will manage this.

INDUCED LABOUR/INDUCTION

Labour normally starts naturally any time between 37 and 42 weeks of pregnancy. The cervix softens and starts to open, you will get contractions and your waters will break.

In an induced labour, these labour processes are started artificially. It might involve mechanically opening your cervix, breaking your waters or using medicine to start off your contractions, or a combination of these methods. In Australia, approximately one in three women have an induced labour.

WHAT ARE THE DIFFERENCES BETWEEN AN INDUCED AND A NATURAL LABOUR?

An induced labour can be more painful than a natural labour. In natural labour, the contractions build up slowly, but in induced labour they can start more quickly and be stronger. Because the labour can be more painful, you are more likely to want some type of pain relief.

If your labour is induced, you are also more likely to need other interventions, such as the use of forceps or ventouse (vacuum) to assist with the birth of your babies. You will not be able to move around as much because the babies will be monitored more closely than during natural labour.

You will only be offered induced labour if there is a risk to you or your babies' health. Your doctor might recommend induced labour if:

- You are overdue (more than 41 weeks pregnant).
- There is a concern the placenta is not working as it should.

- You have a health condition, such as diabetes, kidney problems or high blood pressure.
- The babies are making fewer movements, showing changes in their heart rates or not growing well.
- Your waters have broken, but the contractions have not started naturally.
- You are giving birth to more than one baby (twins or multiple birth).

Not everyone can have induced labour. It is not usually an option if you have had a caesarean section or major abdominal surgery before, if you have placenta praevia, or if your baby is in breech position or lying sideways.

If they decide it is medically necessary to induce labour, first your doctor or midwife will do an internal examination by feeling inside your vagina. They will feel your cervix to see if it is ready for labour. This examination will also help them decide on the best method for you.

There are different options for inducing labour and you may need a combination of treatments.

It can take from a few hours up to as long as two to three days to induce labour. It depends how your body responds to the treatment. It is likely to take longer if this is your first pregnancy or you are less than 37 weeks pregnant.

BREECH BIRTH

This is when a baby presents bottom or feet first. In Australia, approximately 3-4% of babies are in the breech position by the time labour starts. Sometimes a procedure called external cephalic version will be discussed – this is where a doctor gently turns the baby in late pregnancy by placing their hands on your abdomen and gently coaxing the baby around so it can be born headfirst. This turning is done at around 36 weeks, using ultrasound to help see the baby, cord and placenta.

The babies and the mother are monitored during the procedure to make sure everything is okay. There's a small risk that turning the babies may tangle the cords or separate the placenta from the uterus. This is why the procedure is done in hospital, in case an emergency caesarean is needed.

Your midwife or doctor will discuss with you the best way of managing breech labour and birth. If the baby is still in the breech position at the end of pregnancy, a caesarean may be recommended.

NEWBORN INTENSIVE CARE UNIT

You might not take your babies home immediately.

Sometimes, due to unforeseen complications, your babies need to stay under the care of the hospital a little while longer. In this instance, your babies will be transferred to the neonatal intensive care unit (NICU).

The neonatal intensive care unit is the part of the hospital specifically equipped to care for babies who are born with severe medical concerns or those born well before term. They have modern equipment that assists babies in breathing and keeps their body temperatures regulated so that they can continue to grow.

If one or both of your babies are taken to the NICU, you can feel confident that they are getting the best care available. The clinicians understand how fragile those small lives are and want to see them grow strong enough to go home with their parents. You should be prepared, though, for some things that may be a bit upsetting. The babies may be connected to lots of equipment that measures just about every major function. IVs may be inserted anywhere on the body including the feet and head.

You should also expect to hear lots of noises in the NICU nursery. Those sounds keep the staff alerted to how the babies are faring. You will be welcomed into the NICU to hold your babies, and perhaps, even feed them. Breastmilk is still the most superior food for your children. So, though your babies may be unable to nurse, they will be given breastmilk you express for them.

Skin-to-skin is a term you will hear a lot as babies respond well to being placed directly on your skin. This is where your partner can play a huge role as each of you hold one of the babies close to your skin.

Doctors might even experiment with placing the twins together in the incubator to see if it helps them respond better to treatment and feel more secure.

> *One of the most widely circulated photos in the last few years tenderly demonstrates that the twin bond is formed in the womb. A 1995 article in the* Worcester Gazette (Mass.) *entitled 'The Rescuing Hug', described twins born prematurely and put in separate incubators – a standard practice. Three weeks after birth, one of the twins was in critical*

condition; the nurses were unable to stabilise her and feared she would die. With the parents' consent, they put the twins together in one incubator. The healthy twin snuggled up to the sick twin and wrapped her tiny arm around her sister. Within minutes, the sick twin's blood oxygen rates were the best they had been since she was born.

Dr Lynn Perlman, PhD, *Twins Magazine*

When your babies can put on weight for several days in a row and have no acute concerns, they may be able to go home with you. This is good news to some parents and terrifying to others who fear they cannot give them adequate care. But be assured that you will get into a care routine with your babies once you get them home. And your medical team will stay in touch to ensure they are progressing well.

For Birth Plan Template, see Appendix 3.

CHAPTER 6
IT'S TIME TO DELIVER

'Birthing twins unleashes a primal force within a woman's core being that empowers her to transcend the unimaginable and emerge triumphant.'
Annie Gibbins

For the birth of my first set of twins, I went into labour at 35 weeks and rang the local hospital, where I had attended my prenatal classes to inform them I was coming in. As we waited to be put through, we discussed how we had been told that only 1/3 of twins are born vaginally, and we hoped this would be our experience. The midwife in our class had previously recommended we accept an epidural for pain relief. Apparently, it is quicker for the medical team to respond to problems if the mother already has good pain relief, so it's ideal to be prepared. As I didn't yet know if I'd need an assisted birth, I held off on making this decision.

James triple-checked that my hospital bag was at the door and that his personal additions – including our favourite photo, a candle and the music playlist he made with our favourite songs – were all there.

TWINS

To our surprise, they informed us they could not accept twin births under 36 weeks and that I needed to present at another hospital which I had never been to. I was stunned! My calm quickly turned to panic, and after a few frantic minutes relaying the situation to my husband around pausing between contractions, we got the map out and tried to work out where 'King George V Hospital' was.

Before the days of GPS, this was quite an experience as I was not good with reading maps at the best of times, and this was not a good time to improve my skills. But somehow, we made it. I was welcomed in and taken to the labour ward.

After a quick physical examination and monitor of the babies' heart rates, they put me on a drip to stop the labour for a few more days. As you can imagine, I was not impressed as I wanted my babies out NOW! But they kept saying, 'Let's see if we can slow things down a little,' and, 'Every day in utero counts.' They put me on bed rest, hooked me up to a drip, and due to my condition of cholestasis, I continued to scratch like mad.

I'm still not sure whether it was due to my unstoppable tears or an unrelated medical reason, but after five days, they decided to induce me.

Suddenly, now was the perfect time!

After six hours of intense labour and a small crowd of medical students watching on, my cervix achieved its goal of 10cm dilation and Twin One was born, with the generous support of happy gas and my cheerleader husband. A 'perfect delivery', they announced as my son Caleb was checked, wrapped up and popped onto my chest for immediate skin-to-skin bonding.

Then, as the team got prepared to deliver Twin Two and

my husband was given our newborn to snuggle, my situation abruptly became more complicated. Apparently, my body acted like its job was done and my cervix had shrunk back to 4cm. To my complete shock, I was informed that Twin Two had turned transverse and contractions had stopped. James, shocked, asked, 'How on earth do we get the next one out?'

After birthing a 5lb 8oz baby out my vagina, the obstetrician started pushing hard on my abdomen to turn the other baby back into the desired head-down position. I must have been seeing stars or swearing, as I remember demanding an epidural, even though I had previously stated that I didn't want one.

They responded with, 'Sorry, darling, it's far too late for that,' and then I overheard a staff member asking the theatre to prepare for a possible emergency delivery.

WHAT?!

I never imagined a twin birth having one natural delivery and the other by caesarean. How was that not on my list?

They calmly informed me not to worry, as hormones had been added to my drip and I had approximately 45 minutes to deliver Twin Two before we moved to Plan B. Considering I was now approximately 20 minutes post-Twin-One, this delivery didn't give me much time at all, and seeing theatre staff arrive at our door didn't help my focus.

Thankfully, and somehow miraculously, my second son was born 42 minutes after the first. Everyone cheered, he was checked, wrapped and placed on my abdomen. I then made the final effort to birth their fused placentas.

I looked over to see my other beautiful bundle lying in his baby trolley bed and said to myself, *Annie, you are seriously amazing*. Yes, mamas, be super proud of yourselves. We need to change our mindset on what is humanly possible.

My husband James was beaming with pride as his eyes darted from me to the cribs and back to me. He whispered the words, 'I'm so proud of you. You are a legend.'

I accepted this compliment without hesitation and whispered back, 'I'm a superhero,' and, 'We are now the proud parents of TWIN SONS!'

OUR SECOND TWIN BIRTH EXPERIENCE

The second twin pregnancy was similar but different. On the one hand, I knew what to expect with the months ahead and my birth preparation. But, on the other hand, I now had my toddler twin boys who were highly active, and it was very hard to rest. Even though my house looked like it had just been ransacked and I had a strong desire to tidy and clean, by the end of the second trimester, I made sure I took a nap whenever they let me.

As my previously stretched ligaments fatigued and abdomen expanded, my itchy nemesis, cholestasis, returned with vengeance.

For this birth, I was determined to drug up early, get off the table and let gravity give me a helping hand. But at my 32-week obstetric appointment, I was informed both babies had turned breech.

'Are you serious?' I exclaimed. The thought of feet, knees or buttocks coming out first blew my mind for a minute.

The doctor smiled and calmly responded, 'All will be fine. As they are not likely to turn again, I'm going to book you in for a caesarean at 35 weeks.' This was quite a shock to process, as although I knew the chances of a caesarean delivery doubled with twins, I somehow hadn't imagined this would happen to me.

Due to the size and health of my current and pending babies, he agreed to let me deliver them at my local hospital, so I was thankful for this small mercy. Knowing the birth date of our next twins felt weird but it certainly made child care preparations for our toddlers easy.

We prepared a roster around who would assist James in caring for them and prayed they would cope with the changes in routine, separation anxiety and new-found stardom of being big brothers of twins. I must admit, checking into the hospital, getting a spinal block and being wheeled off to theatre to have our son and daughter carefully extracted two minutes apart was surreal.

No pain, no panting, no pushing – what's not to like, right? But as my placenta was removed, it caused a postpartum haemorrhage accompanied by intense pain and bleeding. Apparently, this can occur more often with multiple births, so while I was groaning and going into shock, the highly trained staff responded with the necessary IV fluids, medication and care.

I must be honest with you, recovering from abdominal surgery and significant blood loss, while caring for and feeding newborn twins and keeping twin toddlers entertained and safe, makes everything else I've done in my life feel easy! When people asked me, 'How are you coping?' I'd say, 'Just fine, thanks.' But if I had my time again I'd say, 'I'll be a whole lot better if you cook me a meal, vacuum the house or hang out my washing.'

EXPECT THE UNEXPECTED

When you are giving birth to twins, it is important to keep an open mind. What you think will happen could be very different from your actual experience. The purpose of a birthing plan is not to be rigid. Rather, it enables you to think through what you would like under ideal conditions and gives your medical team a guideline – or better, an ideal – that you want to achieve. But, since twins are unpredictable in every way, I encourage you to be flexible and ready to make changes on the spot under medical guidance.

Your journey will be uniquely yours and it demonstrates the incredible power of your mind, body and soul. Ultimately, the goal is to have two healthy babies, and as the mum, you are ready and equipped for the incredible journey ahead.

CHAPTER 7

WHAT HAPPENS NEXT

'Nurturing the essence of a woman's soul is the secret to her success and happiness.'
Annie Gibbins

Congratulations, you are a mother to twins! Your celebrity status has now been activated, and if you thought life pre-birth was a mammoth journey, your tiny bundles of joy are about to rock your world to a whole new dimension.

POST-DELIVERY

After the birth, your midwife will examine the placenta to determine if you have identical or fraternal twins. If one or both of your babies require special or intensive care, you will be transferred to a more specialised hospital. If not, you will spend the next few days learning how to feed, bath, change and care for them. And the new baby smell and cuddles you will be blessed with! OMG newborn babies are divine!

Not long after childbirth, I experienced intermittent bleeding as my uterus was recovering from its epic role in my children's arrival. I also noted some changes to 'down there', which set off quiet alarm bells. I was questioning, 'What is happening to my body?'

Following delivery, it's not uncommon during the first few weeks to experience bleeding from your vagina, which may appear as a heavy, bright-red flow, with or without clots. It should not smell and can last four to six weeks. Some women have period-like pain for a few days as the uterus contracts, and it can feel stronger while breastfeeding. You will want to drink plenty of fluids and eat a high-fibre diet to ensure your bowel motions stay soft and don't cause unnecessary discomfort. If you have a tear, stitches from an episiotomy, varicose veins in your vulva or just feel swollen, you may hesitate on opening your bowels for the first three days.

All you can do is be brave, don't strain and breathe through it. Make sure the staff are aware if you haven't gone by day three as they will give you some medication to assist the process. Bathe the sensitive area with clean warm water as it will help it to heal, and nursing staff will guide you on the best way to manage perineal care. You may need to sit down gently or lie on your side more, so find out what works and know this time will pass quickly.

DISCHARGE PLANNING!

You will be discharged when the hospital believes you and your babies are ready to go it alone, and this time frame differs significantly from person to person. For some parents it's three to five days, others spend weeks splitting their time between home and hospital with one or both twins.

This is an extremely challenging time for individuals and couples to navigate, especially if they have other children to care for or a lack of support from friends and families. To minimise the feeling of overwhelm and exhaustion, accept any offers of help made by the hospital, family and friends that you find beneficial to your personal circumstance.

The early weeks after delivery will present a lot of fluids coming out of the vaginal area. You will need lots of pads and a plan for how you will change and dispose of them in a sanitary fashion.

Considering what you have been through, it's completely understandable that your body needs to be cleansed and time to heal.

WAYS YOUR VAGINA WILL CHANGE AFTER GIVING BIRTH

I wish that I had someone to talk to in the earlier days, or resources to read, when it came to things 'down there'. Your body has gone through a massive process, and your vagina has done a lot of the hard work. Understand that, after birth, your vagina and body in general will take some time to bounce back. You may feel drier down there, and if you had an episiotomy during delivery, you will have significant healing and aftercare required.

During pregnancy your body is firing with oestrogen and other hormones, causing an elevated level in your body. After birth, these hormones can dramatically drop. It is the presence of oestrogen that acts as a natural lubrication. If you are experiencing discomfort, apply a lubricant. If any pain persists, please consult with your health care professional.

YOUR VAGINA AFTER PREGNANCY MAY BE A BIT WIDER (OR IT MAY NOT BE)

Your vagina is designed to enlarge during birth, and typically, will bounce back to its original size and elasticity. However, this can take a little time, so be patient. If, like me, you temporarily have additional leakage during basic activities such as laughing, jumping or sneezing, get obsessed with exercising your pelvic floor muscles daily. These hidden muscles support the uterus, bladder, small intestine and rectum, and are the secret to keeping everything tight in all the right places. I was all for that ASAP, and they do work!

YOUR VULVA MIGHT BE A DIFFERENT COLOUR

Your vulva may be bruised following birth, or even a different colour depending on any pigment changes during pregnancy. While some of these changes can be frustrating to experience, try to remember that there is nothing wrong or untoward. Your vagina went through a completely natural change after doing something pretty incredible. Please never feel too embarrassed or concerned to speak with your partner, support networks or health care professional.

CHAPTER 8
TWIN FEEDING

'Breastfeeding twins is the perfect combination of safety, security and sustenance.'
Annie Gibbins

After you give birth to your twins, assuming there aren't any complications, the first concern you will probably have is feeding them.

In order to get enough milk to feed both babies, I encourage you to commence breastfeeding as soon as possible. Feeding two babies at the same time is quite a feat, so see if the hospital offers support from a lactation nurse and make an appointment for them to watch and correct your attachment.

I remember the shock I experienced as my milk came in around day three and my breasts started swelling to gigantic proportions. It felt and looked like I had breast implants, so be prepared for this added size in your maternity bras and clothing.

If your supply kicks in rapidly like mine did, the engorgement can be quite painful, but it will settle down, so push through. Try wrapping chilled cabbage leaves around your swollen breasts – the cooling effect works a treat!

Breastmilk works on the supply-and-demand principle. The more your babies feed, the more milk is made, so don't worry about having enough as your body will respond to your babies' feeding demands.

Whether you end up feeding them at the same time, expressing or a combination of both, be obsessed about protecting your posture and nipples. For example, with my first twins, I got told to feed both at the same time. I quickly found my back ached and my nipples got shredded by poor attachment. I then changed to feeding one after the other, or when 'desperate', half-fed each and then finished feeding one whilst burping the other. If my husband James was available to help, I fed them together, whilst James experimented with various positions until I found my way.

Breastfeeding should not be painful and is a beautiful time to bond with your babies as they grow. It is extremely important to ensure your nipples are kept soft and supple so avoid soap or heat to avoid them drying out and becoming cracked.

Another tip is to alternate breastfeeding one twin and bottle-feeding the other with previously expressed breastmilk. If you put the express pump on one breast while feeding the other twin, you can capitalise on the let-down and then preload the next bottle of liquid gold. I had one twin who fed in 20 minutes while his sister took 40 minutes, so it's important to adapt your regimen as required.

I quickly learned it was a higher priority to be positioned on a comfortable and well-supported chair with pillows and nipple shields in situ, prior to starting a feed, even if it was tempting to self-sacrifice for a crying newborn.

Once you have one bottle prepared with breastmilk or

formula, it can take the pressure off times when both are screaming, or when one feeds more than the other. Whatever anyone else tells you, the only right way is what works for you. Just remember to keep drinking water as you are now giving out a lot of fluids and it's easier to get dehydrated and contract bladder infections, such as cystitis.

If you are opting to bottle-feed, preparation is key. Make sure you have your bottles and teats sterilised ahead of time, so it's quick and easy to add your formula and water. A sealed container with spare bottles, teats and pacifiers will save your sanity when the babies are crying and needing speedy attention. It's always great to have a team of two when you are bottle-feeding, although it can be done by one person by carefully propping babies on pillows. Make sure you have everything you need before you sit down as you never want to leave them unattended while feeding.

Mastitis is a condition causing inflammation of breast tissue and is caused by a blocked milk duct or a bacterial infection, causing inflammation and pain. To minimise the risk, wash your hands thoroughly before each feed. If your breasts become red, painful, hot and tender to touch, or if you have flu-like symptoms with a temperature, please consult with your health care professional immediately as you will need to treat it sooner rather than later.

CHAPTER 9

PREPARING TO GO HOME

'I may not know what I'm going to do next but I'll lean into the future I desire to inherit and pray the universe supports me.'
Annie Gibbins

You would chuckle quite a bit watching my husband and me as we left the hospital with our twins for the first time. We were thrilled to be leaving the bright lights and antiseptic smells of the hospital. But, I have to admit, we would miss the skilled nurses who knew everything about babies. It just didn't seem right that they were releasing us to survive in the wild. Sending two young parents home with two babies without a 20-volume manual telling us what to do felt risky!

YOU NEED INFORMATION

All kinds of questions cropped up in the first days of being home with the babies:

- Do they sleep separately or together?
- Should they sleep in cribs or bassinets?
- Where should I position them in the crib?
- What if they cry a lot?
- How much reflux is too much?
- To swaddle or not to swaddle?
- What if one baby has a fever?
- When should I call the doctor about a concern?
- What is the right temperature in the house for the babies?
- What if a baby doesn't want to eat?
- How do I take care of that weird thing where my babies' umbilical cords used to be?

We realised that it was not unusual to have lots and lots of questions. All new parents do. The more we read and talked to our family, friends and other parents of twins, the more relaxed we were and the more competent we felt in our abilities.

We made sure we had the most important basic safety concerns down pat, and beyond that, we allowed our knowledge to grow over time. We also gave ourselves permission to ask any question we needed answers to before we left the building. The doctors and nurses did their best and assured us all would be fine. After all, they were used to dealing with nervous parents.

In addition to frantic 'phone a competent friend' phone calls, there is plenty of information for you to consume – both helpful and unhelpful. That said, I went on the hunt for books, videos and stories of twin parenting as not many people had the answers for some of our niche questions.

I wondered why information about such an important topic

wasn't in one cohesive space, one blog or a single book where women could get all sides of this amazing experience and make informed decisions.

That is why I decided to write this book to make your journey and that of your loved ones easier as you bring your babies into the world.

WHAT DO NEWBORNS REALLY NEED?

It is a reality you can't escape: babies need stuff. And twin babies need lots of it. But make sure you refer to my New Baby Checklist in Appendix 2 before you go too crazy shopping.

We were fortunate to have friends and family who generously loaned maternity clothes when I was pregnant, and lots of furniture, supplies and baby clothes after my children were born.

We even turned to the members of our church to get help with donations. Lots of what we received was brand new with tags still attached because people overspend when preparing for new babies, and babies grow faster than our ability to dress them in all their new clothes.

Anything you can get that is new or in great condition will help to protect your budget and ensure your babies have everything they need.

With twins, everything is volume, volume, volume. A case of nappies or diapers, for example, barely lasts a week. When one baby can go through five to ten diapers daily, twins can empty a box of diapers in no time. You'll need double and triple of everything.

YOU NEED YOUR BABIES TO BE SAFE

It is always best to start baby-proofing your home as soon as you find out you are pregnant. You do not want to wait until your belly is big and your thoughts are geared toward delivery. Experts recommend you start baby-proofing in the room where the babies will spend the most time. That will probably be the nursery. Then work your way out until you have covered every room in the house. Remember to think from the mind of a baby. No height seems unscalable to them after 12 months, and they grow fast!

For the first three months, we focused on providing a quiet, warm home with their bassinets side by side in the middle of the living room as it was directly outside our bedroom door. Once they moved to their own room and relocated to their cots, we focused on keeping them safe by minimising blankets and toys within their reach. As we progressed to turning over, crawling, standing and leaping, we constantly reassessed the potential dangers and adapted as required. For example, you need to be careful that heavy objects like bookshelves and TVs are not going to tumble over.

For us, placing things up high only seemed to spark their curiosity. We found it best to store things that were dangerous, valuable or easily breakable where they couldn't access them. The garage, attic and basement are good choices if the doors to these places can be locked. Less is more! In other words, it is better to have an emptier room with less to tempt than a room filled to the brim with hazards.

First time around we had Caleb 'the climber' and Daniel

'the taster', and from the moment they were mobile we realised turning your back for a minute could result in unpredictable, and at times, very challenging outcomes. Caleb saw every object as a mountain to be scaled, including his cot at age ten months and our neighbour's fence at age 18 months. The triumphant grin he gave as he reached his summits with the bravery of a lion without an exit strategy left us laughing and crying on many occasions. Daniel, on the other hand, preferred to learn by taste and put anything and everything in his mouth. You wouldn't think a child would try eating sand, palm fronds, batteries or Lego until you have 'that child'.

Second time around, while our boy twins fine-tuned their unique gifts and talents, Sam 'the explorer' and Hannah 'the actress' started to craft theirs. Sam had a knack of quietly wandering off on his own adventures resulting in many frenzied moments shouting, 'SAMMMMM WHERE ARE YOU?' while holding back tears as my mind imagined worst-case scenarios. His sister Hannah was always close by and loved to put on theatrical shows, which involved props from around the house including sheets, kitchen utensils and mummy's high-heel shoes.

As you can see, my baby-proofing was a constant journey of adapting to our changing needs. One Christmas, when some presents 'accidently' got opened (by no-one who wanted to confess), we found it easier to put the tree in the playpen and add the presents last-minute than deal with the constant present 'checking' and 'touching'.

ANNIE GIBBINS

YOU'LL NEED TO TIGHTEN YOUR PURSE STRINGS

The financial impact of having two sets of twins was one of the most jarring realities we faced. There are no two ways about it: babies are expensive. It is almost as if manufacturers know that we will fork over grand sums of money to give our babies the best of everything. But, unless you are independently wealthy, twins are going to hit your bank account like a tsunami, so get savvy about trimming the fat. Manage your expectations and try not to lament over what you don't have or can't afford. Cancelling unnecessary subscriptions and researching what you need two of is a great place to start. For example, our twins only slept in their bassinets for three to four months, so we could have put them straight in their cots if we needed to avoid the associated double expense of this item.

The great news is that young kids are not focused on money as they live in the moment. They really just need a good mix of love, time, sustenance and fun to sparkle. Due to our age and available resources, we had to find ways to make every dollar stretch, and when you get creative there are many ways to make that happen. For example, for years we purchased no-name bulk food at the supermarket and preloved clothes at op shops. We took daily trips to the park where there was always fresh air, playgrounds and lots of other children to interact with. In Australia, we were able to purchase a discounted annual zoo pass which gave us weekly adventures 'into the wild' where they could run, climb and explore to their hearts' content, and ideally sleep all the way home.

TWINS

In addition to the zoo being great for children, it was contained. So even if we temporarily lost Sam (which we did – on one occasion), we knew he'd be somewhere in the zoo.

There were certain entertainment venues we avoided for the most part. Movies, for example, were a luxury, and going to the surf was stressful. So, we became very creative in finding daytrips and holidays that didn't cost much money.

We also sourced rental accommodation on a wide variety of farms so our kids could have active holidays collecting eggs with the farmer, swimming with turtles in country dams and riding their pushbikes around the property. Our kids never knew our financial situation back then and were perfectly happy playing on fences near sheep, cows and deer and occasionally being offered a pony ride.

Do what is possible.

What you can't do, you can't do. It is best not to dwell on the state of your budget. We accepted donations, were thankful for gifts, worked our budget and looked for ways to cut costs. We put the emphasis on being together, rather than what we were doing when we were together.

We are blessed today that our five adult children are pretty self-sufficient, resilient and content. Though they are all creating their own path in life, they are not constantly chasing money to make themselves happy. Happiness, not reliant on money, is a skill they learnt as a family when they were young. Doing the ordinary made the special events really special.

I can speak from a place of confidence now, but I vividly remember thinking, *Are we going to be poor forever?* It seemed like the days of stretching our money, seeking out discounts and making sacrifices would never end. But they did. As the children got older, we had more options and were able to work on our financial life.

As the years go by there will be dance lessons, swim club memberships and horseback riding fees. You may want to contribute to their college funds or send them to private schools. But in the first few years of your children's lives, I encourage you to keep it simple and enjoy the limitless priceless moments that are readily available at no cost at all.

FLEX YOUR CHEF SKILLS
Making your own baby food can save you immense amounts of cash and is healthier for your babies. With homemade baby food you have less waste, and you can control the ingredients that go into your babies' bodies, especially sugar and salt. Some super smart parents figured out that you can pour baby food into covered ice trays. So, when it is time to move your babies to solids around six months of age, buy yourself a food processor, acquire new puree skills and start experimenting with a range of fruits and vegetables that can be prepared in perfect portions to cook, freeze and thaw with nothing wasted.

EARNING MORE MONEY
This is a dicey one. You can always look for ways to increase your income. However, taking a second job or working overtime means more time away from home and away from the babies during their formative years when both parents are needed. Is there a way to find the right balance? Many parents look for work-from-home opportunities, which are abundant in today's

economy almost anywhere in the world provided a decent internet connection is available. This new gig economy allows people who have skills in graphic arts, proofreading, web development and thousands of other business areas to take on individual projects they can complete from home.

ASK FOR WHAT YOU NEED
If your friends and family want to buy you gifts, it would help if they bought you what you actually need. Be specific with your list including season and size for clothes. You don't want ten newborn baby jumpsuits and none for them to grow into. Considering their size changes approximately every three months, it's worth being specific. A personal registry ensures that you get the right quantity of the things you actually need, so be bold in your requests to family and friends.

While there is a lot of research going on about twins, there is very little that spans the entire lifetime of twins, following their stats over decades. Research is being helped by the increased amount of attention twin studies are receiving. Additionally, there are more twins being born now than ever due to fertility interventions. In fact, as of 2021, the number per capita of twins is higher than it has ever been in recorded history.

Even with the boost in the number of twins, there are still less than two million twins born each year. That's just over 2%. So, know that you are still in an exclusive group of parents who share many of the same struggles.

1991
———

Busy Busy

1993
———

Crazy Busy

2000
———

Insanely Busy

CHAPTER 10

REMEMBER THE ENVIRONMENT

'The future our children inherit will reflect the environmental choices we make today, so we better choose wisely.'
Annie Gibbins

It is common for new parents to become more aware of the way they impact the world. They worry about how their babies might be affected by dirty water, mounting trash and filthy air, and seek out environmental statistics[1] that motivate them to become better stewards of the land they use. Even if this is not a hot-button issue for you, you can find lots of ways to reduce waste and be kind to the earth.

For example, plastic or cloth diapers. Diapers and wipes are some of the most environmentally unfriendly items you can purchase, as they require a lot of toxic chemicals and waste a lot of water in their manufacture.

---

1 sciencealert.com/becoming-parents-makes-us-25-percent-less-environmentally-friendly-says-new-report

On the disposal side, diapers fill landfills in every country where they are sold and find their way to places they are not. The harmful chemicals that are used to make them leech into the ground and decrease the purity of groundwater. All waste eventually makes its way to the oceans, lakes, rivers and streams that we depend on for clean water and food sources.

The level of plastic in the ocean is a growing global concern. Current estimates suggest that there will be more plastic in the ocean, by tonnage, than fish in 30 years, at the rate trash is being dumped there.

To measure the impact of diapers around the world, consider just the United States, where four million babies are born each year. If each of those babies uses an average number of diapers, he or she will use 2,000-2,500 diapers in the first year of their life. That amounts to *trillions* of diapers thrown into the trash, and that's just from birth to age one.

Babies usually wear diapers for two to three years, though they use less and less each year. But it gets worse. It takes a single diaper several hundred years to decompose. That means that we are still coexisting with the diapers from our years as a baby.

And we are still living with the diapers that were used when our parents were babies. Imagine that!

Then there is the issue of placing a substance filled with chemicals next to our babies' tender skin.

Diapers require the following chemicals to be made:

- Tributyltin.
- Dioxins.
- Adhesives.

- Dyes.
- Perfumes.
- Sodium polyacrylate.
- VOCs (volatile organic compounds).
- Plastic.
- Polymers.
- Phthalates.
- Petroleum.

The good news is that there are good alternatives to toxic diapers. The bad news is that they don't usually stock these at local grocery stores, and they tend to be more expensive and less convenient to use.

BIODEGRADABLE DIAPERS

These diapers are manufactured to break down more quickly and easily. The bulk of the diaper is made with bamboo and few harsh chemicals.

CLOTH DIAPERS

The most common challenges of cloth diapers are:

- Smell.
- Rashes.
- Laundry.
- Leaks.

If you are comfortable managing these, this tried-and-true ancient method for baby waste is still a great option today. There are environmentally friendly diaper covers that go on top of the cloth diaper so that the babies' clothes are protected.

Many people have done cost comparisons of buying and washing cloth diapers, as compared to using a laundry service to pick up and clean them. Cloth diapers win in most cases.

If you wash them yourself, cloth diapers win 100% of the time. As for wipes, opt for reusable washcloths over disposable wipes for the less messy diaper changes.

I'll leave this decision up to you!

CLOTHING

Environmentally friendly maternity clothes are definitely a big option for eco-conscious mothers these days. While it can be hard for people to make the decision to consider the environment above fashion in their day-to-day lives, pregnancy is a great time to do so as you naturally glow as you grow.

Your maternity clothes are usually meant to cater more to function and comfort than prepare you to walk the red carpet at the Academy Awards to get that Oscar you so richly deserve!

You can buy gently used clothing which greatly benefits the reduction of manufacturing and clothing trash. After your babies are born, you can keep the cycle going by donating your gently used and environmentally friendly clothes to another expectant mum.

While cotton is the preferred fabric for clothing, it is also the most harmful, using millions of gallons of water and lots of chemicals to produce. Sustainably grown cotton is a great alternative as these manufacturers follow rigid standards to protect the earth.

REUSABLES

As I shared, we were beyond lucky to have a family, church and community who came running to the rescue with all kinds of gently used baby items. This was a great help to our strained budget. But, just as importantly, it kept those items out of the trash and put them to good use. That was great for the environment. Babies grow so fast that parents hardly have time to use many of the things they buy or receive as gifts.

Unless it has been soiled or damaged, it is great to reuse these items from trusted friends and family members. Check all baby equipment to ensure it is sturdy and safe. Children's items are sometimes recalled when the manufacturer, government or concerned parents discover a safety issue. You should check any pre-owned equipment to ensure that it is safe to use.

You can do this by checking for recalls that have been issued in your country. Within Australia, Product Safety Australia[1] are best known for tracking products recalled, or in America, source information from Recall[2].

---

1 productsafety.gov.au/recalls
2 recalls.gov

CHAPTER 11

SELF-CARE IS ESSENTIAL

'Self-care is not selfish. It's an essential part of ensuring you remain the person you were born to be. Thriving, not just surviving.'
Annie Gibbins

Once the babies arrive, you won't be able to do everything you used to do – or at least the way you did before. Although you would walk to the ends of the earth and fight the biggest lion to protect your children, it's not worth it if you die in the process. Your number-one job is to recover and not to strive for your former life. Your recovery is paramount. It may sound selfish, but it is one of the most loving things you can do for your new babies. Love *you,* so you can love them more!

Liken this part of your parental journey to the emergency safety instructions you hear as a flight is on the runway about to take off. The flight attendant will instruct you to put the oxygen over yourself first, so you can then help your child. Childbirth is no different. The stronger you are, the better you can care for your babies. You will need to establish a new normal that now includes two babies. I cannot stress enough how important it is to prioritise your recovery as you navigate your new life together.

Giving birth is one of the highest acts of service a woman can give to the universe. What could be more impactful to the world than adding another living and breathing individual? The contributions of that one child could change the lives of hundreds, thousands or even millions of people.

So, after giving birth, learn to be okay with respite and recovery. Trust me, creating life is enough.

Don't allow yourself or anyone else to pile on chores, work, business, stress and other responsibilities. I am a firm believer that we teach people how to treat us. We set the expectations. New mothers need to alter their language and begin to speak clearly about how much they are looking forward to their recovery time. This communicates to everyone in their space that they will not be available the moment they give birth to resume all of the activities of life from prior to the babies' arrival.

You also need your support crew to help take care of you! Your natural instinct will be to ensure the babies' care comes first. Your support system needs to zone in on your care as well, to ensure that you are eating well, resting often and healing from the delivery. In essence, they care for you so you can care for your beloved offspring!

They may also need to help you for a while in getting back and forth to the bathroom, which you will have to do often in the early days. If your doctor has recommended you take special care, don't try to make it to the bathroom on your own because you don't want to be a bother. You should rely on them to run errands to keep you and the babies stocked with supplies.

If you are a particularly neat person, you will be troubled by your inability to clean. Ensuring that you have planned for who will clean the house in the first couple of weeks is important. If this is not something your postpartum support person can or will do, hire a cleaning service if your budget allows or reach out to the Salvos or your local church for assistance. Do everything possible to keep housekeeping to a minimum as it is not your priority at this time.

Self-care also involves feeling good about yourself so please do not get stuck wearing the same thing every day. You will feel more energised each time you refresh and put on clean clothes, plus it reminds you to have a shower!

Allow your support people to rub your back or feet and help you do your hair. We may call these self-care actions luxuries, but they are essential to your overall wellbeing. In truth, they are important all the time, but they reach critical importance after giving birth.

As you sink into the beauty of the postpartum process, be sure to maintain an attitude of flexibility around all the things that are happening. Each birth experience is different. Even if you have other children, this will be a unique experience. Just as every childbirth is different, every postpartum experience is different.

Everything may not go the way you expect, so try to get into a flow state that allows the situation to run the way it wants or needs to go.

If you focus on the wrong thing during this time, your outcome will be skewed, and it may feel more challenging than it needs to. Set your mind and heart only on what you and your babies need during this time. Focus on healing, nursing, bonding and being loved.

Many women start to think about how pregnancy has changed their body. I loved my new fuller breasts, but that pouch in my belly messed with my head. But, considering the size my body had stretched to while pregnant, it was completely normal to have more skin and less tone post-delivery. It is not normal to expect your body to instantly snap back, and pictures of celebrities implying it does do women of the world a major disserve. It took nine months to get to where it needed to be and will take a decent amount of time to find its new balance. Pregnancy impacts almost every bodily system, and while most pronounced are the changes you can see, there are also changes that you cannot. The hormone surges that were necessary to accommodate three people must now return to accommodating just one. So, if destructive self-image paradigms try to take residence inside your head, I encourage you to have a direct conversation with them and cast them out.

Your body needs time to heal.

That same flexibility also refers to your emotional state. There will be days when life feels euphoric and glorious. Bask in these moments. You will look over at two amazing babies and marvel that you were able to carry them, feed them and birth them. They are home and safe.

But there will also be days when life feels overwhelming and unmanageable.

Feel that as well. Rest with that. Don't rush to do something to change it right away. Your inner self is also healing which includes fluctuations in mood and hormones. Allow yourself to feel the full spectrum of emotions. You are not 'supposed' to feel anything in particular. All of your emotions are valid.

The fairytale of the perfect mum holding her perfect baby and surveying her perfect life is just that – a fairytale moment. As they say, 'Comparison is the thief of joy.'

For some parents, life before pregnancy might have been fragile, and the birth of twins represents major change in every area of their life. If you were planning for one baby, or none at all, the surprise of two can be daunting. Marriages or relationships may have been tenuous prior to the pregnancy, and they fear what may happen next. Others may have financial or health concerns. Each woman has her own bowl of lemons from which she is working to make lemonade. Your emotions will reflect that.

While I was blessed to have someone in my life who could hear me and respect what I needed, this is not always the case. Be kind to yourself and set boundaries with those around you. Be sure they understand that you will need to discuss all that you are feeling. Without question, you want to have honest and open discussions with your partner at this vulnerable time as you need them on your team.

DISABILITY AND RAISING TWINS

One of the most daunting aspects of parenting is if you or your children have a disability. While there are formal support systems in place to bolster your journey as a new mum, it's vital you seek support – financial, practical and emotional – to help you cope day to day. The path to parenthood will have many more obstacles, but you and your twins will discover the ways that work best for you.

SOLO PARENTING

Not always do we have a partner close by. You may have recently separated from your spouse or opted to raise a child alone. You will need your support system more than ever, so do not hold back on being specific about your needs. Know that you are resilient, determined and designed for motherhood. You can 100% do this!

LONG-DISTANCE CO-PARENTING

Perhaps your partner works overseas, serves in the military, frequently goes on long business trips or works long or unsociable hours. You may feel like a single parent, despite being in a relationship. Communication is key. Explain to your partner if you are struggling and enlist the help of your friends and family. You don't need to 'muscle' through the mayhem. If you feel it, say it.

YOUR EVOLUTION

People use the phrase 'bounce back' a lot. You don't bounce back from a tough time, you grow back. The same is true of giving birth. While it is wonderful and magical, it is tough and taxing. You need time to grow back. The great news is, just like pruning a plant, you will grow back better, faster and stronger than you were before.

BE INTENTIONAL

What you leave to chance will occur haphazardly. You may or may not be happy with the result. But what you plan has a better chance of matching your ideal. Planning is never a guarantee of success, but it increases the probability tenfold. So long as your plan is flexible, you will find that planning helps things run a bit more smoothly.

CHAPTER 12

ESTABLISHING A ROUTINE

*'Your future success is a direct result of
your daily habits and routines.'*
Annie Gibbins

If you think you are doing nothing more than feeding, washing and napping, this is completely normal. Besides making sure you attend appointments with your local baby health centre nurse, clear the calendar and focus on establishing a routine that works for you.

I always made my appointments in the afternoon as mornings for us were bedlam with feeding, bathing and chores taking hours. Besides getting the babies weighed and measured, I found myself in a better headspace to openly discuss the babies' health, routines and hot topics like breast engorgement, contraception and a husband asking when it's safe to have sex again, later in the day.

While you may not be lying awake at night thinking of wild

lovemaking sessions, especially if you had an episiotomy or caesarean, it's important to have a comfortable environment for all things personal.

In the weeks immediately following childbirth, I experienced some regular bleeding as my uterus healed. I also noted my vagina was drier and understandably more sensitive in the early weeks post-delivery. While my body took longer to heal post-caesarean than natural delivery, we are all unique, and our first intimate experience postpartum should be whenever we feel physically and mentally ready. It is therefore essential that your partner understands how you are feeling and any concerns you may have during this time. Most obstetricians recommend waiting six weeks to allow time for full internal healing to take place. This lessens any risk of tears or infection. While some couples reconnect earlier, and others much later, you want to make sure you have fully considered birth control and take things gently. Be prepared to giggle as your breasts spurt milk across the bedroom during moments of arousal.

CHAPTER 13

LET GO OF PERFECTION

'We are all a work in progress and perfect in our imperfections,'
Annie Gibbins

I cannot stress this enough: routines are critical for parents of twins. Routines allow you to manage the never-ending to-do list. And routines help your babies settle into a daily schedule. Routines are essential for everyone.

The biggest routine parents attempt to establish is the all-important sleep schedule. When your babies fall asleep, it's a great time for you to get some rest too. It's tempting, during those quiet times, to do housework, laundry, pay bills or make phone calls. However, many parents swear by the adage, 'Sleep when your baby sleeps.'

There is no way to tell how long a nap will last. A soiled diaper is enough to wake a soundly sleeping child, and if one of the twins starts to wail, it is likely to be enough to wake the other.

So, even if your babies only nap for 30 minutes, take the opportunity to rest and replenish yourself. Besides, there is little in life more satisfying than crawling into bed in the middle of the day.

If you are concerned about sleeping too soundly to hear the babies, invest in a baby monitor to help amplify any sounds coming from the nursery. Or invest in a super-comfy reclining chair that you can place in the nursery for those quick naps.

Should you put your babies in their cribs or bassinets at nap time?

The experts say yes.

After a good meal or a long playtime, you have a good chance of having two sleepy babies.

It helps to make bedtime a part of a larger routine. If you put the babies in the bath, do a baby massage with lotion, dress them in comfy pyjamas and play soft music, they will grow to associate that routine with bedtime and fall asleep easier when they sense the routine has begun. There are no guarantees that sleeping babies will stay asleep, but at least try and get the evening started right, with both babies asleep at around the same time.

Now that we have covered a bit about schedules and routines, it is important to inoculate you against something that often bedevils parents. It is the scourge of perfectionism. You love your children and want to be a terrific parent. You hope to have everything in place and in order so that you can properly care for your kids. You never want to run out of baby wipes or turn over the baby lotion bottle only to find it empty. You want your kids to be clean, well-dressed, well rounded and well-behaved.

But the quest to get everything right can morph into a kind of perfectionism that can cripple new parents. Expecting to get everything right sets you up for certain failure. Because no-one is perfect. Even with all the money, staff and resources in the world, twins can find a way to throw a serious monkey wrench in your best-laid plan.

So, relax. Go with the flow.

There are no mistakes. There are only learning experiences. And there are unlimited opportunities to laugh at yourself and the crazy situations you navigate. Managing the learning curves will not be easy. So, setting the standard at perfection is intentionally setting yourself up for failure. I failed many many times, so don't worry, this one is a learning curve.

I remember the day I was feeling completely impressed with myself by getting my kids ready for a party in their best outfits, but as I arrived at the destination, I smelt disaster. One of the children had experienced a diarrhoea explosion which had leaked into their beautiful clothes and proceeded to then seep into their car seat. I then remembered I'd left the baby change bag at home and gasped. By the time we returned home, changed clothes and then returned to the party, most of the event was over and I was completely frazzled. When James came home and said, 'How was your day, babe?' I just burst into tears and walked away to take a long shower. Those moments are humbling, to say the least, and do take a while to recover from. But the sun always rises the next day!

I am naturally task oriented, so I saw everything as a project that needed to be completed on time and correctly. Everything was on a schedule because I wanted to do it all right.

I learned to ask if it was even right for our family. And when it wasn't, I had a new task to learn: how to say 'no'.

PRACTISE THE WORD 'NO'

If you are like me and enjoy spending time with friends or going to family gatherings, you will notice almost immediately that it takes special consideration to accept invitations to various events. You will remember how easy it was for the two of you to get dressed and get out the door on time. Suddenly, going out is a major production.

There are bottles to be prepped, baby food to be packed, supplies to be checked and loaded in the baby bag. Then there is the pram or stroller that needs to be placed in the car. Sometimes there are two!

At first, we would accept most invitations. But that became exhausting, so on occasion, we had to comply with the words, 'Thank you, but no thank you.'

Letting other people down is okay if that is what is best for your family, especially when you are stressed at the thought of trying to get out of the house and the kids are overtired.

This will only be for a short time. As your children get a little older, moments of freedom become a little easier to seize.

There are the logistics of actually getting everything packed and everyone in the car. I remember having to put four sets of shoes on every time we went out. Sometimes the biggest challenge was just to find ones that matched. Whew! It was exhausting!

If you add any complicating element like bad weather, other children or a case where one of you can't go due to a work obligation, the task gets exponentially more difficult. And the time of day is always a major consideration. If the event is longer than an hour or two, you have to consider where you will put your babies down for a nap, change their diapers and feed them.

Coming home early has to be an option. Even if you have the time of your life at the event, you still have to drive home, move the babies inside and unload the car when you will probably be exhausted from the gathering.

There are some events that you cannot say no to. Your grandma's 90th birthday party might be a must. But the yearly summer barbecue might have to be a no this year. Telling people 'no thank you' when they extend an invitation will not be easy at first – for several reasons.

Firstly, if you want to go, you will be disappointed that you can't. In addition, some people don't have an appreciation of the herculean operation required to get out of the house with twins.

Secondly, in our case, we had two sets of twins. So, everything quadrupled. We had to accept invitations carefully. I still have flashbacks of that moment when the Sunday school teacher told me my three-year-old daughter didn't have any underpants on. I was mortified at the time, however, on reflection, it was a good indicator of how hard it was just to get there on time. Most people understood, but we got a bit of pushback and it hurt.

THE BABYSITTER QUANDARY

You might hear from well-meaning people who insist that you come to an event that you should just get a babysitter. I often chuckle when I think about it. What 16-year-old is capable of taking care of twins for four hours, let alone two sets? And how much would a qualified nanny cost?

One day, when Caleb and Daniel were around two years old, we asked my in-laws to mind them for a couple of hours so we could attend our friend's fundraiser being held at a hall up the road. While we left them quietly sleeping, we returned to a very stressful scene. Caleb had taken his soiled nappy off and had chosen to spend nap time fingerpainting on the walls around his cot as Daniel quietly slept. We arrived to my father-in-law greeting us donned with rubber gloves and a bucket in hand. They quickly shared that Caleb was in the bath and their room needed 'urgent sterilisation' and raced out the door as soon as they could. Not surprisingly, future babysitting was hard to come by.

When the twins are babies, you may have to rely on an extended network to help, however, it is wise to be cautious about who cares for your twins outside of you and your partner in those first few months. This is especially true if your twins were low birth weight or had other complications.

You may need to hunker down for the first few months until they are old enough and strong enough for limited visits outdoors. Getting them minded by someone else is the ultimate trust, so choose your sitter wisely.

BECOME A FAN OF SPONTANEOUS FUN

Don't get so stuck in a routine that you lose the ability to be spontaneous or do something random. You may be driving along and see a fun one-time event happening in your neighbourhood, but you look at the time and notice that it is close to nap time. Do you stop or not? I would always recommend leaning toward the special event.

It does mean an unscheduled stop and unloading baby buggies from the car, but I have found the times we took to seize these special moments of fun with our children were almost always worth it. James and I look back with fondness at the times we ditched our plans to make a snowman, slide down grassy hills on cardboard, watch a litter of kittens be born or huddle together as a wild storm passed over.

As time passes, the ordinary gets forgotten but the extraordinary gets etched into our minds and treasured forever, so remember to take time out to build memories you will cherish forever.

CHAPTER 14

THE TEAM EFFORT

*'Your support crew provide a fuel that
never burns out.'*
Annie Gibbins

It's super important to ask, 'Who is on my team?' Of course, you'd like to think that it is you and your partner against the world. But, you might find that the world of raising twins is a whole lot bigger than you imagined. You might want to recruit some additional players onto your team, and that's okay too.

If I had to choose two words to summarise the first couple of years of parenting twins, the words would be 'accept' and 'help'. Although it was clear that it would be much better for me, my husband and our children if we allowed our wider community to pitch in once in a while, I did struggle with this key concept the first time around. I felt protective of my precious cargo, and I also wanted to look like I had everything under control. By the second time around I was accepting help from anyone who offered! There really isn't room for an ego in a family of six, at the time, and later, seven.

You are not alone. Over the years, I have heard many parents discussing their self-sabotaging behaviour and question why on earth they burn themselves out so often. Society teaches women that asking for help is a sign of incompetence or weakness, and this needs to be called out and challenged. The truth is it takes a village to raise a family. Friends are designed to be there for each other during the key transition points in life. There is immense value in the tribe.

We live in the most technologically connected era in human history, yet somehow, we feel more disconnected than ever. Advances in social media and smartphone technology mean you can share with the world your beautifully plated meal at a fancy restaurant, but not the difficult days.

Really, does anyone care what you had for dinner? Most people don't. So, why have a social network if you can't be social?

Twins are so adorable that they become your golden ticket to free help, so learn to trust those in your 'real' backyard, and those knocking on your 'real' door. And let's face it, what's not to love when it comes to help whilst raising a brood like mine?

TELL YOUR TEAM WHAT YOU NEED

Although you may think it's obvious how a dear friend could help you, unfortunately your mental list doesn't always leap out at them. While most people want to help, they may be reluctant to offer as they don't know specifically what to do. They are seriously staring into a foreign land without a map or the language to navigate it. They certainly don't want to intrude on your family bonding time, and they are probably not confident they can add much value due to their lack of experience with twin babies. They don't realise how welcomed they would be, so it is up to you to tell them.

Here is how the conversation usually goes:

Friend: Hi, I heard you had your babies. How are they?
Mum: They are great. We are so thrilled.
Friend: Well, if you need anything, let me know.
Mum: Okay, I will.

This is a perfectly lovely conversation, but this does not give either party what they want and need. The friend wants to help; the mum needs the help. How do we move from a nice gesture to something more concrete?

Let's try a more direct approach:

Friend: Hi, I heard you had your babies? How are they?
Mum: They are great. We are so thrilled.
Friend: Well, if you need anything, let me know.
Mum: That is so kind. If you would be willing, I'd love to get some help next week. Is there a day that would be good for you to come for a short visit?

Now the friend feels useful. They know there is something they can do and have an assignment they can fulfil.

They will be there next week with bells on, ready and willing to pitch in.

Perhaps you noticed the words 'short visit' in my little example above. I put that there for a reason. It's important to set boundaries for visitors. After all, if they come and stay too long, it can have the reverse effect.

The benefit is not just to you and your babies. The people who get to help you also get to bond with your children. They have a place in your family's story that they will treasure. The more people you have who love and adore your children, the better!

So, once you get past *why* you should accept help, you can turn your attention to the *how*.

To that end, I would say that communication is key. People can help better when they know what help is needed. There may be some things that you would prefer to keep private. Perhaps you are private about your bedroom and would not want to have someone help with a task like changing the linens on your bed. That's perfectly fine.

At the same time, you might not want to ask your mother to take out the trash. The good news is the to-do list is so long, there will never be a shortage of ways another pair of hands can help out. I had a whiteboard jam-packed with a rolling list of tasks, just in case I had an offer!

My friends and family loved to come over for a couple of hours, find something on the list they could do, and take care of it in short order. They got such pleasure in erasing that task off the list knowing that they were a help to the people they loved.

I love this quote: 'Many hands make light work.' This is an old saying you have probably heard from your parents. But it's true. You can really define your community by allowing them to come to the rescue at this important time.

'Asking for help isn't always easy, but delegating tasks and having another set of hands to assist is key to surviving life with two newborns. Twin dad John recommends having a system in place to handle parenting responsibilities, which helped him and his wife, Jen, raise their 21-month-old daughters, Angelina and Sophia. 'My wife and I are a team, so we need to share the work,' says John. 'I bathe the girls while she dresses them. Before bed, I make their lunches for the next day. We alternate who does the dishes. Sometimes one parent will take on more than the other parent, and you need to communicate so it doesn't impact the marriage.'

For single parents raising twins, relying on grandparents for support can be critical during those first few weeks. Single mum Lehar Samadhi temporarily moved in with her retired mother and stepfather when her twin sons, Raj and Axl, were born. 'My mum was a tremendous help during the newborn phase,' says Samadhi.

So, get the board mounted on the wall. If you live in rented housing and can't hang something, you can simply tape poster boards to the wall. The point is to make clear to people all of the things that need to be done and let them choose how they want to help.

If something is urgent, you can highlight it or mark it with a star so that people know your most pressing need. Just be sure to keep the list up to date.

You don't want people doing a chore that has already been

---

[1] todaysparent.com/baby/newborn-care/real-life-parenting-hacks-for-raising-twins

done. The vacuuming, for example, may be a tough call visually. If your best friend already vacuumed for you early in the day, you don't want your aunt to do it again in the afternoon because it was not crossed off the list.

SAMPLE LIST OF THINGS PEOPLE CAN DO TO HELP

Take out the trash.
Run the dishwasher.
Bring over a meal.
Put a load of laundry in the washing machine.
Give a baby a bottle or a jar of baby food.
Vacuum the floors.
Run a simple errand like the dry cleaners or the pharmacy.
Sterilise a batch of bottles.
Change linens on beds.
Watch the twins for 20 minutes while you take a walk.
Watch the twins for an hour while you take a nap.
Watch the twins for two hours while you get pampered at the hair salon, nail salon, spa or whatever makes you feel good.

SCHEDULING, APPS, CALENDARS AND REMINDERS

There is already too much rolling around in your head so do yourself a favour, avoid the overwhelm and put anything of relevance into an online calendar and make use of home delivery apps. When your babies arrive, there will be so many additional requirements to keep straight: medications, doctor's appointments, mothers' group, baby health centre … and they all take planning.

My advice is to start your week by scheduling in your 'personal' and 'couple' time BEFORE the busyness of the week takes over. Plus, make use of the reminder settings and smartphone alarms! You are the CEO of your own life, and YOU get to determine how you spend your time, money and energy.

While I had to ask James to make a quick stop at the supermarket on his way home from work, if it was today, I'd arrange home delivery to get him home quicker. Similarly, many diaper services have apps that will allow you to set and adjust your diaper pick-up and drop-off days, as well as adjust the quantity easily as the children get older.

The list of electronic devices for new parents seems endless. There are baby soothers, video cameras, electronic rockers and a host of other gadgets that can help. Just check reviews from other parents and online, and make sure the price is worth the potential benefit.

The older and wiser I have become, the more time I block out for my non-negotiable needs. Sleep, personal time, exercise, date nights, family celebrations and holidays are all essential and therefore need to be prioritised. Around work and appointments I also block out preparation, travel time and a buffer before the next activity. If I don't do this, it's easy for my time to get hijacked. There is so much value in establishing, maintaining and communicating your availability, role and boundaries in all aspects of your life. It is easy to say yes and worry about the practicalities later, but the end result will be others taking advantage of you, intentionally or unintentionally, and that never works out well. Remember, we all have 24 hours in a day, so ask yourself – *How am I going to use mine?*

FIND YOUR TRIBE

Other mums, particularly other mums of twins, are invaluable members of your team. Mums of twins, you can be sure, are experiencing the same struggles you are dealing with. They have had to develop systems that work to keep them sane, and their advice is worth hearing.

You may try something that works for another mum and discover that, for one reason or another, it doesn't work in your household. I recommend that you give new ideas a bit of time to see if the tip doesn't work or if your family just needs some time to settle into it.

You can search in your community to find a group of mums who get together in person or online. If you don't find one easily, try the following:

- Ask your obstetrician.
- Ask your paediatrician.
- Check with the hospital where you delivered.
- Look online for a mothers' group or multiple birth club.
- Check apps like Meetup that are designed to bring groups together.
- Visit your national multiple birth club website and search groups.

TEAM PROS

In addition to your midwife or doula, there are lots of professionals who specialise in the 'baby space'. If money is not a major issue, you can hire a housekeeper, personal chef, night nurse or sleep consultant. Some parents even book virtual appointments with a licensed therapist just to have a safe place to sound off about any struggles they are facing. Make sure you check with your doctor if you can access any free or low-cost services.

Please, never try to go it alone.

CHAPTER 15

POSTPARTUM BLUES

'Postnatal hormones are like being strapped into a roller-coaster without your consent.'
Annie Gibbins

After our second set of twins were born, we were developing a routine that worked most of the time. Not surprisingly, I was constantly overtired and had bouts of weepiness from hormonal changes post-pregnancy and birth. Breastfeeding newborn twins every three to four hours around the clock, while raising very active two-year-old boys, was overwhelming, exhausting and at times lonely while James was at work. The responsibility felt huge, and the demand on my mind, body and spirit was unrelenting.

Not surprisingly, postpartum depression can be quite acute in mothers of twins as the sheer magnitude of the task is enough to make any mum question herself. There is no need to feel ashamed as this is perfectly normal. Talk to your doctor if feelings of sadness or depression last longer than a couple of days, and drop everything and call for help immediately if thoughts of harming yourself or your babies cross your mind, even for a moment. Don't worry that someone will swoop in and take your babies away. Postpartum depression is a known concern, and psychologists and counsellors are highly skilled at helping you through this time while you continue to care for your babies.

Your mental health is a top priority for your entire family and there is absolutely no stigma or shame associated with seeking out professional support and getting help.

FATHERS AND DEPRESSION IS REAL

While postpartum depression (PPD) is commonly associated with new mothers, fathers of twins tend to have higher instances of postpartum depression than fathers of single babies.

Researchers estimate that about 10% of fathers experience symptoms associated with PPD and would benefit from professional counselling.

> *According to a report issued by the US Preventive Services Task Force, 8.9% of all pregnant women and 37% of new mothers experience clinical depression in the months before or after giving birth. (Less research has been done on new fathers, but some studies suggest that about 10% of dads may also succumb to postnatal depression.)*
>
> *But, for parents of twins or other multiples, there's good evidence that the percentage who experience depression may be much higher. A 2009 study, published in the journal* Paediatrics, *found that new mums of multiples were 43% more likely to have postpartum depression than mothers of singletons.*

In a survey published in May in the Journal of Psychiatric Practice, *parents who'd had at least one multiple birth told researchers they experienced the most difficulty during the first three months of their babies' lives. For that study, 244 parents of twins and other multiples (including 197 mothers and 44 spouses or partners) completed a series of questionnaires that asked about their mental health during the postpartum period. (About 2/3 of the kids in question were over age five at the time their parents were surveyed).*

The researchers found that although 48% of the study participants had struggled emotionally after their babies were born, few got help.

Juli Fraga, NPR Radio

Your partner may or may not know exactly what you need. It is unfair to judge another person for failing to meet a standard they do not understand and feelings they are not experiencing.

You can share books and videos with them that will help them settle into their role. Be specific with your partner on how they can support you during this time by clearly expressing what would be helpful and appreciated.

Many women resort to the 'he should know what I need' mode. This mindset will only harm your relationship and slow your recovery process. Do not be afraid to simply state what you want and what you don't want.

The study we explored above found that sleep deprivation can exacerbate symptoms of postpartum depression. With parents of twins, the sleep deprivation is multiplied. So, it is not odd to find that parents of twins are at greater risk of PPD. Still, many parents don't let their health professional or partners know that they are having trouble. Don't let this be you. If you or your partner are experiencing any of the following symptoms, seek help:

- Mood swings.
- Anger.
- Anxiety.
- Guilt.
- Hopelessness.
- Loss of interest or pleasure in activities.
- Irritability.
- Fatigue.
- Loss of appetite.
- Unwanted thoughts.
- Inability to concentrate.
- Fear.
- Insomnia.
- Urge to run away.
- Uncontrollable thoughts.

Postpartum depression does not mean you are not or will not be a good mother. It doesn't mean you don't love your babies. Love yourself well and allow yourself to feel what you feel. If you need more support, be proactive and ask for it.

It is time to drop the narrative that we should grin and bear it. Motherhood is tough stuff, and often, we need support to make the transition, especially when twins are involved. It is time to do an extraction of that toxic ideology that keeps women feeling somehow broken. You are worthy of receiving help and support.

Together, you and your partner are embarking on a strange and somewhat magical journey. You have been twice blessed. And while you won't get everything right, there is so much to be gained from this wonderful experience.

Sex, for example, may have to be postponed until your body has recovered. You may want to find other expressions of love and closeness that do not require your body to be penetrated at this vulnerable time. Educate, don't berate. Teach him how to love you well during this period and watch your connection grow. Your hormones may cause you to desire sex more or less. Be thoughtful. Ask your partner to let you lead during this period.

Live every moment for the moment. Grow together as a family. And once the difficult days are over, you can look back with your family and laugh at the tough times.

CHAPTER 16

TWIN DADS

'Parenting provides the opportunity to celebrate the essence of who your children were born to be.'
James Gibbins

Annie and I have a wonderful marriage. Always have. Sure, we have our ups and downs, but we are solid, loyal and committed. Watching Annie as a wife and mother makes me immensely proud, and I am so thrilled that she has handed over 'the ink' to me, to share my story about how our twins came into this world.

When we went for that first scan, all of our friends knew there may be a distinct possibility that twins would arrive, because Annie had this glow about her, plus a bulging belly. I remember leaving work to meet up with Annie for our first scan, sitting in the ultrasound room, and the nurse commenting, 'Wow, you do seem big, Annie.' The moment the probe made contact with Annie's tummy, the nurse loudly and clearly proclaimed, 'Congratulations, you're having twins!'

I felt stunned. I was excited on the outside, but on the inside, I was a little shocked, and dare I say, numb. After receiving this mind-blowing news, I returned to work. As my colleagues saw me approaching my office, they all called out, 'Twins?'

I remember being in such a state of shock, all I could do was walk past them in silence. At this point, my silence spoke volumes, and they burst out laughing, 'Yes, I guess it's true. They are having twins!'

Thankfully, the initial shock did pass by the next day, and I was then able to genuinely feel and behave as excited as Annie.

We always wanted a big family.

Like the birth of our first twins, the second was also planned. We always wanted at least four children. But the funny thing about twins is that no-one can plan for them or plan not to have them. They just happen. If you like, they're a 'divine intervention'.

When Annie fell pregnant again, her belly popped out very early, almost mirroring the first twin pregnancy. Immediately, and ironically, the same set of friends and family laughed, 'Wouldn't it be hilarious if you got pregnant with twins again?'

Seriously, you couldn't write it better.

I was not at all concerned it would be twins again. I anticipated that Annie would 'pop out' early, as her body had been incredibly 'stretched' during the first pregnancy. It was not until a few days before our scan that I suddenly felt a surge of cold shivers. I thought to myself, *Surely we won't have* another *set of twins. Will we?*

The second scan was like a re-run of the first. Again, Annie and I headed into the doctors' office for the scan, the nurse, again, commented on how big she was.

Wait for it. Yes, we were pregnant again with our second set of twins.

Gosh, it had somehow happened again. Perhaps lightning really does strike twice! A twin pregnancy is not that unusual, and it's estimated in Australia that one in 80 pregnancies will be twins. But two sets of twins side by side is a rare phenomenon.

Again, I returned to work stunned and shocked, and again recovered fine within a day or so. I was immensely excited and eager to welcome two more babies into our warm family home.

Looking back, having five small children in a family home was daunting, hectic and busy. But for me, I loved it. Annie and I loved having a vibrant, noisy, energetic and lively home. We were fortunate to have five relatively healthy, outgoing and active children who loved games, fairytales, trips to the playground and holidays to the beach. We created, and continue to create, so many happy memories together.

The early years were so special, and I am moved to tears just thinking about how Annie and I made our lives work, happily.

People often ask me, 'So, what was dinnertime like at the Gibbins' household with five small children?' Well, it was like a small party every night. Large volumes of food were prepared, everyone was called to the table together, we all sat in our regular spots and there was lots of chatting and laughter (and of course, some mess).

On occasions we might have had a visitor or two for dinner. They would casually just sit and stare at the chaos quietly, as they asked, 'Wow, it is like being at a party. Do you do this every night?'

I would always respond, 'Yes, and we absolutely love it. We couldn't imagine our lives any other way.'

Sure, having two sets of twins just 26 months apart, and

another daughter six years later, meant life wasn't without its challenges. I may be an optimist, but I am also a realist. The volume of work and the energy required every day was draining at times. I was very conscious that when I went to work, I had it easy compared to Annie's role at home, running our expansive clan. For me, my real work started when I got home in the evenings. There was housework to be done, tiny clothes to hang on the line and toys to be relocated away from the main thoroughfares.

Once a week, I made 'daddy dinner', which ideally involved a barbecue or anything that came semi-prepared, and on Friday date night we added a glass of wine and occasionally ordered takeaway. After washing up the dishes, bath time, playtime, wind-down time, reading time, bedtime prayers time, it was (hopefully) sleep time.

It takes a very strong partnership to do what Annie and I did. Our patience was tested, and happiness, most days, hinged on communication and compassion for one another. But we did it, and we not only grew as individuals but as a couple. We have a bond like no other, and I am just so proud of my wife.

We were blessed, however, with extra gold — our children loved to sleep. I attribute this to Annie's parenting skills (and a little of mine), but Annie was rigid with bedtime boundaries. Every night, we aimed to stick to the same routine, were strict with what time the babies were put down and ensured that every trick in the book for sleep discipline was followed. It was a blessing and a miracle that our twins fed fast and we learnt to nap on demand. Our days were so demanding, but with a good night's sleep, anything felt possible.

Being a parent is, of course, a role that comes with fear. Fears around health, finances and whether your babies live a happy life. One of my earliest memories put my resilience to the test.

Just after we brought the first twins home, Annie suddenly suffered a serious episode of asthma, which required her to be hospitalised for a few days. I was at home by myself with two newborns, and despite being ridiculously under the pump, I was so distracted worrying about Annie. That's the thing with having a family, you don't get to choose when you tap in and out of being a responsible father. I received so much help and support from family and friends, but sadly they couldn't be there for midnight feeds.

I was feeding and changing both babies overnight, every three hours. My cooking, cleaning and wellbeing were taking a major hit, but I did it. I am quietly so proud of myself for keeping our home going during this time.

Fortunately, Annie was able to easily express her milk in the hospital, and before you knew it, I had litres of the stuff frozen in our fridge at home. In fact, because it was being expressed and the babies were being bottle-fed, I was able to measure precisely what was coming out of Annie and what was going into the babies. And you know what, Annie was expressing far more than I needed! The supply-and-demand chain was booming.

She was producing over a litre a day! The boys were healthy eaters, but even they could not consume 500ml each per day. I was absolutely stunned at Annie's capacities. The female body is truly astounding.

Now, I know I am offering a brief and compact version of fatherhood in the early days, because this is Annie's story to tell.

But for the dads out there, know that you are incredible. Your role is different, but just as important, and no-one is a perfect parent, despite what social media would lead you to believe.

Firstly, remember that children only grow in one direction: older. Which means these gorgeous little children will never be at this stage ever again. We need to enjoy every moment and stage to the max, because the chance to enjoy these moments will never come around again. Lots of wonderful, new and exciting stages will come, but early days and younger moments will pass you by before you know it.

And most importantly, remember, you and your partner are on a long-term ride. It may be rocky and unpredictable, but it can also be magical. It is so important to remain kind, thoughtful and keep in mind that you are a team of two doing all of this together.

Annie, thank you so much for writing this book. For sharing your courageous moments, knowledge and love for the world to read. I am without a doubt your biggest fan.

There are some things you can encourage your partner to do to enhance their experience and navigate those disorienting early days of being a parent to twins:

ENCOURAGE QUESTIONS

If they have questions, rejoice. You are blessed to have a partner who is active and engaged. Allow your partner plenty of space to question the medical team about any portion of the pregnancy and delivery.

BE SPECIFIC

Help your partner help you. Specify exactly what you need and give them jobs to do. It is confusing to say, 'I need you to be there for me.' It is better to say, 'Can I have a backrub?' When you communicate with your partner in clear terms, you are more likely to get what you need, and your partner feels like they are really in it with you.

CELEBRATE YOUR PARTNER

I cannot stress enough how important it is to love and care for your partner throughout your pregnancy. You are the one with the baby bump, so you are the one who will be receiving the attention, cheers and high fives. Pass some of that love and acknowledgement to your partner. Make sure they know that you need them and appreciate their love and care of you during this time.

We worked together as a unit from the start, but that only happens when there is mutual love and respect for each person's place in the birthing and parenting processes.

CHAPTER 17

BEWARE OF SUPERMUM

'All mums are superheroes – who else can juggle being a nurse, teacher, chef, cleaner, coach, negotiator, accountant and peacemaker all in one day.'
Annie Gibbins

I will never forget our lovely neighbours and their reaction when we came home with our twin boys. They were a sweet Italian couple who fell immediately in love with our children. But I remember how they praised me for being a supermum just because I had twin boys. 'What an incredible woman you are, birthing two boys; your husband must be so happy with you.' We were deliriously happy to have two healthy babies and their gender did not make them better or worse, so this perspective did not sit well with us at all. It gave me a taste of gender discrimination, and I must admit, it fired up my soul to champion gender equality later in my life.

One day, I was walking down the street and another

neighbour said, 'Here comes supermum,' and I felt an instant discomfort and pressure from their words. What they didn't know, and what most people didn't know, was that I was just hanging on by a thread with all four children covered from head to toe with chickenpox and distressed by their constant itching and high fevers. At that moment, I was extremely unsure of my abilities, and this title put an unhelpful pressure on me to present as better than I was. Once again, their words were meant as praise and the offence I felt was unintentional, but worth noting and reflecting on.

There are times when you just need to put everything on hold, just to stay sane. When the two sets of twins were about four and two years old, there was a particularly fierce storm overnight. The wind howled, and driving rain poured constantly. At about six the next morning, our son Daniel came to James' side of the bed and gently woke him up with the question, 'Daddy, why is the floor all wet?' James opened his eyes, expecting a toilet overflowing or something similar, swung his feet out of bed only to find them splash into a couple of centimetres of water ... not just in the bathroom, but everywhere.

James yelled at me to get up, and to our absolute horror, we found that the water had run throughout the entire house, which was a large single-storey home on a concrete slab. Virtually every corner of the house was saturated. And then our sense of smell quickly alerted us to the next horror. This was not just plain water; it was coming from the sewer!

Amid the panic, we rang our neighbours and rapidly explained what was happening. Then, we asked if we could send the kids over 'for an hour or two' while we worked out what was happening. Next, we woke the rest of the kids and passed them over the fence, in their pyjamas, to our friendly neighbours.

A quick inspection throughout our home soon uncovered the third horror. The source of the sewerage was the floor drains in the bathrooms and laundry, and they continued to spew forth a steady stream of polluted water into the house. Everything we had on floor level and a few centimetres above was contaminated. At this point, we could have both sat down to cry, but we kept our emotions buried and focused on what needed to be done.

We made emergency service calls to our plumber, home insurer and parents. To their credit, and our relief, the emergency service team arrived relatively quickly. They casually informed us that a row of nearby pencil pine trees had penetrated the public sewer line. Consequently, the refuse had backed up to our yard and should have poured out of our gully. Unfortunately, the gully was not able to cope with the huge amount of stormwater entering the system, and the next exit point was in our home.

'What the—?' Now we could sit down and cry! And I did! The experience was completely overwhelming. While the State Emergency Service and plumber attended to the ongoing emergency, other members of their team systematically walked through our home and started throwing everything they deemed contaminated onto a pile in our front yard. The pile rose quickly.

Most of the kids' toys, every single shoe we owned, clothing, kitchen goods and every bit of furniture was buried in that pile. Then the carpet, lino, wardrobes, bookshelves and kitchen cupboards found themselves in the same forlorn fate. 'All potentially contaminated,' the men would mutter.

Over one rainy night and day, our home was flooded, our

kids were evacuated and most of our belongings were gone. A few hours later, we went back to our neighbours and told the kids we had decided to go on an impromptu holiday to a hotel, which was going to be 'so much fun'. While they got excited and jumped about, the truth was we were shattered. We were being sent to a hotel with random items of clothing and had no idea what we would do next.

The next few weeks were completely overwhelming and exhausting, as there was no quick fix, and all sense of security and routine was lost. As we were already homeless, we decided that a fresh start would be useful and decided to sell our house. While adjusting to the new routines of regular school and pre-school, we managed to prepare our home for the sale, bought a block of land and moved five times while the house was being built.

Although I thought we were keeping it all together, I must have looked like a complete wreck as a group of friends came collectively to James and politely, but firmly, suggested, 'You need to take Annie on vacation ... without the kids.' As he shared this 'great idea' with me, my mind responded quickly with, *When? What? And where? Is this even possible?*

James had the answers to all of my questions. Four different families, with kids the same ages as ours, had offered to take on one of our children each. We only needed to find enough money to go away for four days. The idea sounded amazing and exciting, but it also sounded CRAZY! 'The kids will be fine,' our concerned friends assured us. 'You both desperately need this.'

I tried to make James change his mind by telling him all the reasons why our kids wouldn't be able to cope without us. 'We need to save every single cent for our new house otherwise it will never be finished and we will remain homeless forever!' I shouted. I had developed a new habit of crying unexpectedly and then profusely apologising for my tears.

As I sobbed on my friend's shoulder, she looked at me and said, 'You are a beautiful mum who loves her tribe of twinnies to the moon and back. But your body is exhausted, and you need to give yourself a break. The kids will be fine. You must stop and look after yourself.' That was all I needed to hear. No more convincing required.

James arrived home from work with tickets booked for a long weekend at a tropical island getaway and confirmation that the kids were all booked in at their respective holiday houses. 'When mummy's not happy, nobody's happy,' he said. 'Let's get you smiling again!' OMG! Was this happening?

I alternated between feeling stunned, angry, excited and overwhelmed at what this meant and what it would require. But James was clear; we were going. I had not thought of taking time out for self-care or some alone time with James for five years now, and the idea of moonlit dinners, romantic walks on the beach and drinking cocktails by the pool sounded heavenly. Sleep on its own would be sensational. Imagine a sleep-in … every day! To calm my nerves and alleviate my mummy guilt, I couldn't wait to ring the kids before they went to sleep on the first night. To my delight, they all expressed how much they missed us but then went on and on about how much fun they were having on their respective holidays.

'They could sound a bit sadder,' I told James.

'Are you serious?!' he exclaimed. 'RELAX! The kids are fine.

Be kind to yourself. Let people help you. Let's have some fun together.'

The reality was that I had neglected my self-care for years. It seemed there was always something else to do and someone else to care for. But over the next few days, I realised that self-care and couple-time is a necessity and not a luxury. We had an absolute ball, and so did the kids. I cannot tell you how amazing this mini holiday was for our relationship and myself personally.

James came back from the holiday with a new phrase: 'Happy wife, happy life!' Every time I've needed some time out since then, I've quoted the phrase back to him. In the early days, 'time-out' was meeting a friend at the end of our street and going for a night walk after our kids had gone to bed. Later, I joined a gym and used their child care service so I could workout and go for a swim.

From that day, I have deliberately scheduled regular times to invest in myself and my relationship. Now, I love hiking, coffee shops, the occasional massage and regular couple getaways according to time, budget, family and work requirements.

Hopefully, it won't take losing a home you love and moving five times over 12 months to realise that you can benefit from dedicating more quality time to self-care.

There is no medal for pushing yourself beyond normal human limits in parenting. For many years, we juggled two family Christmas celebrations in 24 hours, which resulted in complete exhaustion, tantrums and tears, all at a time when we should have been quietly enjoying our special family moment. James used his saying, 'When mummy's not happy, nobody's happy,' and this was a day that completely bowled me over. The fact we were up until the early hours putting their Christmas pushbikes together using Japanese instructions, while baking, wrapping, cleaning and stressing, didn't help our already delicate mental equilibrium. Next came overexcited boys jumping into our bed at five in the morning, bright-eyed and bursting to open their presents, not to mention the 'Santa Claus carrot check', church, lunch and a dinner filled with tantrums ...

It took us a very long time to speak up and say, 'We can only manage one event per day until the kids get older, so unfortunately, we will need to miss this year or make it another time.'

Seriously, that's all it takes! The reality is that 'others' won't like your choice, and you will feel the pressure to conform, so it's harder than it sounds and it's the reason why we procrastinate. However, true superheroes have self-imposed boundaries, honour their worth and focus on the primary goal. Your goal is to be happy and healthy so you can be the woman you were born to be – no more and no less.

You can get to that place of balance faster by asking, *What does success look like for me?* When you know your own definition of success, you know what to accept in your life and what to reject or postpone. Your values and your goals become your driving forces rather than your unrealistic expectations or the desires of others.

You will be glad to look back on this time and declare to other mums, 'I made the main thing the main thing.' What is the *main* thing? That is really for you to decide. But it certainly revolves around having the family time to keep your family unit bonded. If you try to do everything to please everyone, you may find that you do nothing well.

Mums are, in general, seen as superheroes. We tend to carry the weight of the world on our shoulders without blinking an eye. And it is true that, as a new mum, you often get in tune rather quickly with your babies' needs, sounds, cries and laughs. This symbiosis can trick you into thinking you are superhuman.

But you are *human*. Trust me. Try to enjoy every moment while it's happening without trying to look too far ahead. Plan for the future, but live in the present.

CHAPTER 18

FREQUENT FAUX PAS

'Sometimes the only thing on the menu is humble pie.'
Annie Gibbins

The difficulties in life can be viewed as problems, mistakes, cons and drawbacks. I choose to look at life's little hurdles as just that: hurdles. You learn to scale them with style and grace. But when you have twins, people see it as an oddity and often say some of the silliest things. Interestingly, they think that they are the first to think of these quips, when the reality is that parents of twins and their children have heard them all a dozen times.

Here are a few we experienced over the years.

THEY ARE NOT 'THE TWINS'

As a parent of twins, you work overtime to make sure they remain individuals with their own lives, desires, dislikes and identities. But other people will, in a most lazy fashion, refer to them solely as 'the twins'.

With identical twins, it's especially important to give people a nudge to learn their names even if they have a hard time telling who is who.

Interestingly, when your children are young, toddlers even, their friends do a great job of telling them apart. So do grandparents, aunts, uncles and others who don't live in the house but see them regularly. Human beings are quite skilled at picking up on subtle differences like facial expressions and body movements.

For example, my son Caleb had curly hair and Daniel had olive skin. So, our friends called them 'Curly Caleb' and 'Dan with the Tan', to make sure they knew who was who. Some parents of identical twins have other techniques like painting a fingernail a colour to remind them of their name. For example, Penny is pink and Barbara is blue.

So don't let people off the hook by allowing them to define your children solely as 'the twins'. Just politely repeat their names as you point to your children and identify them. People will eventually get the message.

ARE YOU 'THE TWINS' MUM'?

This is a common tactic people use to identify you. They don't bother to learn your name because they can refer to you as 'the twins' mum'. Just as in the faux pas above, I kindly and politely offer my hand and say, 'Hi, I'm Annie.'

WHAT SPECIAL SEX MOVES DID YOU DO TO GET TWINS?

Insensitive, and frankly callous, people will impose on the most private parts of your life by asking if you have any advice for how they can conceive twins. No, it is not a result of multiple orgasms or tantric sex. We were just very blessed!

WHEN CLEARLY YOUR TWINS ARE NOT IDENTICAL

Hilariously, I was occasionally asked if my boy and girl twins are identical. I thought to myself, *Gosh, where do I start?*

OKAY. DON'T TELL ME, LET ME GUESS

The amount of fun people have trying to tell twins apart is inversely proportional to the amount of fun you have watching them do it. Lots of twins and their mums complain about this silly little game of 'guess which twin is which'.

At parties, it can be frustrating to your children if they get subjected to the guessing game more than once. You can spare them the annoyance. It is perfectly fine to interrupt the guesser and simply point out who is who. Perhaps respond with, 'You don't have to guess, I don't mind reminding you. This is Caleb, and that is Daniel. So, how are you doing today?'

LET ME GIVE YOU SOME ADVICE

People who don't have twins will give you advice on having twins. It's baffling, I know, but it happens. But unless you have had twins, it is virtually impossible to understand what it's like to manage this unique type of parenting.

There are considerations that simply never come up with parents of single-born children, no matter how many they have.

When people attempt to give you advice, there isn't much you can say without being offensive. It's best to just nod and smile with grace. Listen, absorb and move on. You can enjoy a wicked inner smile at the thought of them with frazzled hair and clutching a bottle of wine after an evening babysitting your twin toddlers.

I'LL BE OVER TO HELP. IN FACT, I'LL STAY FOR A COUPLE OF DAYS

I have strongly advocated for parents to reach out for help. People want to help, and you need the help. But when people come to help and stay too long, it becomes more of a hindrance than a help.

Even very outgoing people, like me, who love to have friends and family around, can grow weary of company that stays too long. Even if the guest is the most wonderful visitor, helps out as promised and offers great adult conversation for the parent, or parents, there does come a point when you want your privacy back.

So, how long is too long?

The answer is: you decide.

But there is a caveat: decide before they arrive. Nothing is worse than having to ask someone to leave when they came to be helpful. So, it is best to decide upfront how long guests will be staying. Or better yet, tell them upfront how long you want them to stay.

Mothers, best friends, aunts, grandparents and siblings are the prime candidates for overnight visits. If your home can accommodate an extra person (or people), you should clarify upfront the length of the visit. Avoid vague terminology like 'a few days' because it inevitably invites misunderstandings.

It can be as simple as, 'We are so excited that you will be coming next week. Would you be able to stay for three days?' Then you and the other person are clear on the expectations. Your parents, or your partner's parents, might want a longer stay. In that case, it might be best to suggest a hotel or Airbnb nearby so that they can stop by a few hours each day to visit, but you can still have your privacy at night.

You can always blame it on the fact that the house is crowded with baby stuff. After all, what home with twin babies isn't?

DO YOU GET LONELY BECAUSE YOU'RE NOT A TWIN?

My second daughter, who is not a twin, has had to deal with people who feel obligated to point out her singleton status as if it is odd. She handles this comment by factually stating, 'You know, 97% of births are single births.' The look on their faces is priceless and makes me giggle. She was born six years after her next brother and sister. She is her own person. She is a testament to what it means to be a non-twin in a family filled with multiples. Her older siblings adore her and make sure she doesn't miss out on anything.

WHAT IS YOUR BABY'S CORRECTED AGE (IF BORN PREMATURELY)?

This is the golden question most parents are waiting to hear the answer to. When you're judging whether your premature baby is developing normally, it is important to understand their corrected age.

The corrected age is your baby's chronological age minus the number of weeks or months they were born early. For example, a six-month-old baby who was born two months early would have a corrected age of four months.

This means they may only be doing the things that other four-month-olds do. Most paediatricians recommend correcting age when assessing growth and development until your child is two years old, when imbalances have usually evened out.

DON'T KNOW WHAT TO SAY

Sadly, while the chances of experiencing the loss of one or both twins are lower than any time in history, some babies do not survive. The grief of losing a child is possibly the most harrowing aspect of a complicated pregnancy. If the unthinkable happens, grief counsellors should be accessed to help you and your family process the loss you are suffering.

Whatever the circumstances, the domino effect of a lost pregnancy or child is felt by all, and people often don't know how to respond. They may unintentionally act awkwardly, say something inappropriate or avoid you altogether. Times of raw emotion can unearth feelings and words that have been deeply buried for a reason. Opening old wounds or being suddenly immersed in the foreign land of grief can cause us to feel ill equipped as to how to move forward. It's a time to be kind to each other, even when that's incredibly hard to do. It is never healthy for blame, shame or guilt to find their way into the grieving process. Life is complex and messy. I encourage you, if you are accepting any feelings of loss, directly or indirectly, feel the feelings. Feel the pain.

But please grieve and heal together.

CHAPTER 19

DOUBLE TROUBLE

'I always worry when they are quiet; something tells me it's too good to be true.'
Annie Gibbins

Parenting twins is a random assortment of mishaps, near misses and injuries. It seems like one child is a handful, but twins are two armfuls, and they sure do keep you on your toes.

As I mentioned, Sam was our explorer and he could figure out how to get lost just about everywhere: the zoo, beach, grocery store, you name it. If there was any way to escape, he found it. Considering you are bound to have at least one child adamant to explore the world, never be casual with safety.

Caleb got so up close and personal with his birthday remote-control car that the wire got stuck between his teeth and we couldn't get it out. As his gums started to swell around the metal intruder and his little teeth disappeared, we took him to our local hospital with his car attached to his face. Much to his disappointment, the doctor used wire cutters to get them separated and tears flowed all the way home as his new car was now broken.

One rainy evening Daniel decided to give Sam a small push while walking along a metre-high railing, resulting in a screaming child with a lacerated tongue lying in a flowerbed in the rain. I hurriedly bundled my pyjama-clad tribe into the car and sped to the hospital as Sam struggled to speak and started flipping his tongue into abnormal positions. As James raced in to meet us at the emergency unit, the doctor announced, 'This injury is quite nasty, Mrs Gibbins, so we will be taking him off to surgery to get that tongue fixed.'

We had our fair share of broken bones, dislocated shoulders, viruses, head lice, worms, snotty noses, coughs, colds and allergies. With five children, it seemed we were at our local medical centre so often, they could have named a wing after our family. Thankfully, the medical staff always understood that 'random things' happen to children.

Once, Sam came to me complaining of a stomach-ache. It got worse and worse as the day progressed, until we decided it was best to take him to the hospital. The doctor insisted it was food poisoning, whereas I was sure it was appendicitis. After issuing test after test, no evidence of food poisoning was found. My son's health deteriorated, and our family got increasingly more distressed. You can imagine the unbalanced power play between me – the young nurse and mother – and the paediatrician with 30 years of experience.

After days of watching my son rolling around in pain and becoming more and more lethargic, I just knew it wasn't food poisoning. Exhausted and consumed with fear, I had a complete meltdown in front of the medical team. I then picked him up with a drip in his arm, and against the doctors' orders, discharged him and drove him to another hospital. I remember sobbing all the way and praying that he didn't die en route. As I flew into the next emergency department, they saw my distress, took my son from my tired arms, and within an hour, confirmed he had a ruptured appendix and required emergency surgery. In order to recover from surgery, treat severe peritonitis and an infection, he remained in hospital for five more weeks. It was the scariest time of our lives.

We nearly lost him.

In addition to the stress of having a child seriously ill, we still had a house filled with other healthy children to care for. It was tricky to navigate because the rest of the family still had school, dance eisteddfods, soccer games and birthday parties. Life still needed to tick over. We wanted home, after all, to resemble normalcy, to help them cope with their brother being away from home for so long.

It was a complete nightmare.

Thankfully, he recovered fully, and we were able to bring him home. I breathed a huge sigh of relief, wiped my brow and thanked the heavens that this ordeal was over.

However, I should have known better. It was, in fact, far from over. The day I brought my son home, his brother complained of the same symptoms. I am embarrassed to say that we assumed he was faking them for attention.

We suspected that he saw all of the attention and care his brother got and wanted to get his share. But after a few hours, it was clear that he was either in pain or the world's greatest child-thespian. We rushed right back to the hospital with our second child suffering from appendicitis, and he was operated on a few hours later.

TWINS

None of us have it together all of the time. We put on our game faces when we go out, but behind the scenes, we are all juggling a lot of balls and hope no-one notices the effort involved to keep them moving. We hope and pray they don't come tumbling down at an inopportune time, but sometimes they do, and those moments can be funny, embarrassing or brutal, depending on your mindset and circumstances on any given day. Just remember, storms do pass, and tomorrow is a fresh new day. Take a moment to breathe, rest and replenish your reserves. You are amazing.

CHAPTER 20

INDIVIDUAL THOUGH BORN TOGETHER

'Twins may have shared a womb but they are always beautifully unique.'
Annie Gibbins

Identical twins occur when one fertilised egg splits in two. It's still a little bit of a mystery as to why nature decides to do this. But identical twins do not, as far as we know, occur because of a genetic predisposition. That is why your chances of having identical twins are low. Even though twins result from the same sperm and egg, they each develop independently, except in rare cases.

Fraternal twins occur as a result of a phenomenon called hyperovulation, where a woman releases two eggs instead of one for fertilisation. It tends to be genetics that predispose some women's bodies to engage in this hyperovulation, and therefore, it can run in families.

It's important to note that fraternal twins each come from their own egg. Having fraternal twins is like having two distinct children belonging to you and your partner at the same time instead of years apart. Just as you wouldn't expect two siblings to be identical, neither should you expect that of your fraternal twins. They look different. Act differently. Think differently. In fact, some fraternal twins even have different skin tones. If you had two partners around the same time, they may even have different fathers.

While some twins are born within minutes of each other, some are a significant time apart.

The longest interval between the birth of twins is 90 days, in the case of Molly and Benjamin West, dizygotic (fraternal) twins born in Baltimore, Maryland, USA, to parents Lesa and David West (all USA) on 1 January and 30 March 1996.

> *Molly was born three months premature on New Year's Day, but doctors stopped Lesa's contractions so she could carry Benjamin for as long as possible.*
> **Guinness World Records**[1]

When twins are born days apart it always captures media attention. In 2021, twins were born five days apart, but it was just long enough for them to have birthdays in different months:

> *Heather Perry never thought the babies she was carrying, scheduled to be born in May, would enter the world in such a crazy, unpredictable way. In February, 25 weeks into her pregnancy, her water broke. She was hospitalised, and*

---

[1] guinnessworldrecords.com/world-records/67465-longest-interval-between-birth-of-twins

weeks later, labour began ... Baby girl Olive was born 24 February, nine weeks early. She weighed 2lb 4oz ... But Olive's twin, baby boy Ashton, wasn't ready to be born, so the doctors decided to wait. 'Every time I would hold her, he would kick around in my stomach, like he just knew that she was up there, but he was enjoying his extra space to sprawl out,' Heather Perry said.

Five days later, on 1 March, Ashton finally entered the world. The gap means the twins will celebrate their birthdays not only on different days but in different months. 'It's going to be a good story to tell at school, and everyone they meet they can tell that story to,' Chris Perry said.

WDAY-TV

The vast majority of twins are born around the same time, usually within minutes of each other. But that doesn't mean that they are destined to share everything in life from that point onwards.

Twins can be as different from each other as any other two children in a family. Even identical twins have different fingerprints. It's a tiny reminder that we are all exceptional, and making comparisons, even with twins, is an unnecessary pastime.

As a parent, it is key to adjust to life as it evolves for the purpose of a child's happiness and wellbeing. Treating each of your children as individuals is a sign of absolute respect.

When our twins went to school, we chose for them to go to the same school and to start in the same class together. For Caleb and Daniel, this worked well as they quickly made new friends and progressed through the learning milestones. When Sam and Hannah started two years later, the same did not occur, as they were a lot more co-dependent. Hannah adopted a motherly role with Sam and happily finished his work and spoke to the teacher on his behalf. It didn't take long for the teacher to call us in and suggest that for Sam's best interest, it might be better if they were put in separate classes. When Hannah responded to the news with, 'Well, who is going to bring home his notes?' we knew this was probably a good idea for Sam's development. They could still sit together at lunch but they needed to independently learn and grow. Over the coming years, Caleb and Daniel moved to an academically selective high school and Hannah went to a performing arts school. These decisions were all huge at the time but were made around their unique differences and needs.

Like all parents, we only had eyes for our little darlings. We cheered them on with raucous applause as they participated in athletic carnivals, concerts and school plays. They all had very different gifts and talents, and sometimes it took a while to find out what they were. We comforted them when life didn't feel fair and they wanted to run away and hide. We hugged it out when one twin was invited to a party and not the other. Our hearts melted when they smiled back at us as they stepped up to their next challenge, believing they could nail it.

A study[1] conducted in 2003 by Dr Eric Turkheimer, who teaches psychology at the University of Virginia, found remarkable differences between identical twins. His study showed that even the IQs of twins raised together vary wildly, just like the IQs of fraternal twins.

The takeaway here is to celebrate their start in life together. But celebrate, also, their individuality. The sheer utility of doing

---

1 smithsonianmag.com/science-nature/brief-history-twin-studies-180958281

things together is hard to resist when you are the parent of twins. In our family, before we knew better, our twins did most things together. They were enrolled in the same schools, registered for the same sports and even wore the same clothes. But it bears repeating, having twins should not be seen as having two versions of the same person. Because they are not, in any way, the same person.

This may seem obvious to you, and by now, you may be wondering why I am harping on this very topic. But I can tell you that it is very easy to forget this mantra when you get into the grind of daily life. It is always easier to drop them *both* off at a karate club, without thinking that although one twin loves karate, the other is just tolerating it. It might be more convenient for you, as the parent, to make the one trip. But your timesaving can, in fact, cause long-term disruption.

Discovering that one of your twins would much prefer an art class on the other side of town presents a new set of issues. Despite the logical issues, I encourage you to never settle for one twin's interests over the other. It takes careful planning, and often, the help of others to get it all done. But it is important for each twin to have their interests nurtured.

As you think about spending time as a family, plan events with the following configurations in mind:

- Time with the entire family.
- Time with each one of the twins separately.
- Time with non-twin children in the family individually.

You can spend an hour or two doing something special with

one twin while your partner spends time with the other – then a week later, switch.

You need the chance to get to know your twin children independent of their sibling. The best way to do that is to be alone with them. This can be tough when your schedule is already jam-packed, but it's so pivotal in a child's development.

The good news is that you can do this in conjunction with other activities you have planned. For example, while Caleb and Daniel were at soccer practice and Hannah was at her dance lesson, I made it my weekly 'mother-and-son' date with Sam. We only had an hour, so he chose the activity. One week it was catching tadpoles, another it was a walk in the park with an ice cream in hand. We even found a life-sized chessboard once which was very exciting! It didn't matter what we did as long as it involved laughing together and connecting on a deeper level. This bonded us to each other independent of his twin.

TWIN IDENTITY

But the best way to stave off twin identity issues is to treat them as individuals, and this can involve reflecting on if their clothes, haircuts and hobbies match their interests and personality.

Some twins bond more closely than average siblings and even speak in terms of 'we' rather than 'I'. Others state that they feel incomplete when they are not with their twin, as if their sibling is the other half of their personality. Others become polar opposites and choose to strongly claim their unique path in the world. We chose to nurture our twins' identities through the following techniques.

TALK ABOUT HOW YOU WERE ABLE TO TELL THEM APART WHEN THEY WERE BABIES

All children love to hear their baby stories, but for your twins, these stories can serve as reassurance, as you tell them about how they arrived in the world differently. Remark about which one loved to sleep versus the other, who was always awake in the crib. Talk about who was fussy and who was calm. Talk about who laughed a lot and who had a serious expression. Your children will enjoy the laughter that erupts from these stories, and this will help them form a clear understanding that, although they look alike, they are, in fact, very different.

POINT OUT FEATURES THAT ARE DIFFERENT

Identical twins are not truly identical in every way. In fact, studies suggest[1] that the DNA of each identical twin is actually different from their sibling. The study found an average of five mutations, or differences, between identical twins. One can have a disguised feature, while the other does not. One might have slightly lighter or darker hair. One may suffer from asthma, while the other doesn't. It helps your twins to secure their identities by pointing out their differences in a jovial and distinctive way.

How to dress them is a personal choice. My preference was to dress them differently. Whilst there aren't any scientific studies to point to, anecdotal evidence reveals twins should have their own clothes and style. Firstly, dressing twins separately helps others identify them and see them as individuals. It also helps to further identify them in photographs and videos. If you employ child

---

[1] livescience.com/identical-twins-dont-share-all-dna.html

care, it can be beneficial to remind your nanny, 'Jake is wearing the green shirt today.'

As they get older, it offers each twin the autonomy to discover their sense of self through style. This enables the twins to flex their fashion muscle, as they decide what clothing best represents who they are. You might be thinking that this will exacerbate your budget because you have to buy an extra wardrobe of clothes. In fact, it's totally the opposite. Buying two sets of clothes is the more expensive option. Giving each baby their own drawer of clothes allows you to separate what belongs to each twin (and share).

> *If parents treat twins as a unit, it can hinder the process of attaining an individual identity, even for infants. To the extent parents can experience and treat their multiples as individuals, the greater will be their children's ability to experience themselves as individuals. The more individuated each multiple is, the more stable their relationship will be throughout the trials of life. Developing as an individual is not a threat to the twin bond, but contributes to the health of the twinship.*
> **Dr Lynn Perlman, PhD,** *Twins Magazine*

It's imperative that you value each child as their own person. Sure, they shared a womb, a birthing experience and their bond is special, however, from birth forwards, they are two separate human beings. Give them room to spread their wings and fly, even if they fly in different directions. When you set out the fingerpaints, you might find that one child plays happily for a long time, while the other gets bored after a couple of tries, and that's okay. Be prepared to offer them blocks, trains, dolls or something else to explore where their interests lie.

CHAPTER 21

JUGGLING BABIES AND DREAMS

When I was a little girl, I was blessed to spend time with two extremely different women. Baroness Irena De Schultze was born in Russia, and Mary Montgomery in Sydney. Born on opposite sides of the world, these two women could not have been more different. And they were my grandmothers.

Irena was born an aristocrat in Russia. She enjoyed the niceties of life, was loud, eccentric and just a tad naughty. Although her mother and sister died when she was young, and her family lost their wealth, title and class when fleeing the Bolshevik revolution, Irena acted like she was still entitled and therefore asked for whatever she wanted and believed it should be forthcoming. She would have been a huge advocate of the laws of attraction.

Mary grew up poor in Sydney, Australia, and was a quiet, reserved and conservative woman. Raised by relatives after her mother ran off with another man, she knew she had to strive hard for everything she needed. Mary didn't dare ask for anything, she just knew she needed to work harder and more strategically to achieve what she wanted.

Both were intelligent, pioneering women who needed truckloads of courage, strength and resilience to rise above their circumstance. Both learnt at a young age they needed to make their own magic happen.

I was inspired as they shared little gems around how they made choices to boldly rise above their circumstance to achieve success on their own terms.

And I would like to emphasise the words 'on their own terms' as this looks and feels different to all of us as we navigate our own circumstances.

When I was a teenager, I wanted to be a businesswoman. Businesswomen were very impressive to me. In my mind, they got to wear nice clothes, enjoyed expensive holidays and politely asked people to help them make big things happen. My clothes were ugly, I had only holidayed in one place and definitely loved to boss people around, so this was my dream job.

Being the passionate woman that I am, I announced to anyone who would listen, 'I am going to be a businesswoman,' and not surprisingly, they laughed at me. One day, my dad told me I didn't have the necessary 'financial head' for business and my mother added I wouldn't be 'a good mum' if I pursued my crazy ideas. So that was it, really – my bubble was well and truly burst.

Although I believed strongly that I would have the aptitude for business and couldn't imagine not being a loving mum, these limited-belief blanket statements resulted in me believing I was not good enough, and I decided to do nursing rather than business at university.

One day, when I was whining about how sad it was that I couldn't become a businesswoman, a shift happened in my mind. My grandmothers had way more challenges in their lives than I did, so what would they say about me spending my precious time and energy entertaining negative thoughts of jealousy, envy and resentment of others?

Although I was now a nurse and not a businesswoman, and had four beautiful children and no money, I dared to dream I could still make my own magic happen; I just needed to find out how.

Irena would have said, 'If you really want the diamond, you have to believe you are worth receiving it.'

Mary would have said, 'If you really want something, then stop complaining, put your head down and work hard to make it happen.'

They were both right.

I needed to stop accepting criticism from other people as a truth and start listening to those who have been ahead of my journey and not behind. So, I wrote down the words 'I have high-level managerial skills' and put them on the fridge, like an old-school affirmation. The family laughed and said, 'No you don't,' and I replied, 'One day you will see – I do.'

I had to ask myself, *Do I actually believe I can one day be a CEO?* Just like an athlete imagines themselves on the winners' podium, did I see myself happily in the role, doing the job and being great at it?

Irena needed the confidence and tenacity to learn five languages and gain university qualifications while raising three children around a world war, immigrating to Australia and then forging a professional career so she could rise above their circumstances. Mary needed pure diligence and dedication to study hard and gain a qualification in accountancy over many years of night school while raising three children as a single mother.

Who was I to not believe the impossible can't be made possible? Even if it took a very, very long time and regular groans of frustration!

Because I couldn't afford the business program, I enrolled myself in a Master of Education, and once a week, I went to university and did assignments after everyone went to sleep, and finally, I was qualified.

A few years after that I became the head teacher of nursing and then a national manager of the orthopaedic surgeons program.

One day I looked back at my fridge and said, 'I do have high-level managerial skills,' and one of my boys said, 'There's no doubting that!'

With this renewed confidence and confirmed skill set, I enrolled and completed a variety of business courses and then boldly applied for and gained my first CEO position.

Since gaining this role and those that have followed, I now look back and reflect on the many steps I have taken to make my own magic happen around a large family.

At first, they were tentative steps, and now, they are full-bodied leaps. Every step required me to dig deep and push through self-doubt and ignore the naysayers, of which there were many.

It was hard at times but always worth it.

I learnt key principles on my journey to 'have it all' and pass them on to whoever finds them valuable:

- Words are immeasurably powerful so use yours to empower others and lift them up.
- Never underestimate the skills you can learn in the most unusual circumstances.
- You have to believe your dream to achieve its blessing.
- Set a goal so big that you can't achieve it until you grow into the person who can.

The narrative of your story is powerful. And it is *you* and only *you* who has the permission to write your own masterpiece.

I had a dream to be a businesswoman, while being a great mum. Against all the odds, I achieved this goal and so much more. I now coach women all over the world to make the impossible possible. My style is a combination of my grandmothers and incorporates my unique quirky side. I ask for and expect the diamonds, and I work tirelessly and collaboratively until the no becomes a yes.

I measure success on my own terms and against my own values.

I am enough.

We are all enough.

So, who do you really want to be?

Write your heartfelt, non-negotiable response down and put it boldly at the centre of your vision board or fridge.

I invite you to start positioning yourself so you are expectant and ready to receive blessings that are within your reach.

Don't allow anyone to put out your fire.

Sometimes we just need the courage and support to open a door.

Other times, we need to start opening different doors.

And if you are like me, you might just have to create your own door and be unapologetic if the dust you leave behind upsets some people along the way.

I've always been attracted to people who dare to dream big scary audacious goals and kick serious butt, shout woo hoo and dance a jig as they achieve their dreams.

I hope this is you as you tackle twin parenting with your own brand of confidence and style.

Together we rise.

Annie xo

CHAPTER 22

IT'S FUNNY NOW

'If the twins are alive at the end of the day, I've done my job!'
Annie Gibbins

Having twins is like a daily comedy show, especially in the early years. There are so many notorious tales we share, and today we sit around the table and laugh about things that happened when our children were small.

But I can assure you, time has provided us some distance from those events, and it is that distance that makes it funny.

For example, one day we were looking for Hannah during the half-time break of a soccer match, and when I called out, 'Hannah where are you?' she yelled back, 'I'm up here in the bushes doing a poo!' As a field of spectators stared back at me with mouths open and eyebrows raised, I quickly went and found my darling and then quietly walked us both to the car to escape the embarrassment that was erupting within.

Once on a lovely summer's day, our family ventured out to the park. After running around with them for a while, pushing them on swings and waiting at the bottom of slides to cheer them on, my husband and I sat on a park bench talking about our plans for the rest of the day.

We had so much to do that we decided to divide and conquer. My husband would go for a walk, and I would return home. All that was left to be decided was who would take which children. He said, 'I'm going to take the boys.' Those words still haunt us because, even though it was a simple statement, it was the start of one of the craziest and scariest moments in our lives. With twins, we should have known, nothing is simple.

My husband went in one direction toward the parking lot, and I went in the other. Before I share the mayhem that ensued, I should explain that we distinguished between sets of twins by saying 'the boys' – referring to our first set of twins – and 'the babies' – referring to our second set of twins, a boy and a girl. We made sure to only do this privately as our little shorthand to talk about the children.

When my husband said he was taking 'the boys', I heard that he was taking all of our male children. So, I scooped up my daughter and headed home. A couple of hours later, my husband arrived at home. He walked in, cheerful as always, and I watched the kids file in behind him. I counted one boy, two boys, but where was the third? Our youngest son was missing.

'Where's Sam?' I asked, hoping that a game of hide-and-seek was happening without my knowledge.

'He is with you,' my husband answered. 'I have the boys.'

It only took about a quarter of a second before both of us realised what happened. We had left Sam at the park. It had been two hours, and our little boy was there alone. We rushed to the car and sped to the park, breaking quite a few traffic laws along the way, I'm sure. I imagined the worst. Had he been kidnapped? Had he fallen and gotten hurt with no-one there to care for him? Had he wandered into the street and gotten harmed? Was he hungry, lonely and afraid?

I jumped out of the car almost before it came to a stop and rushed up to the seating area. There was Sam. He had found a kid's birthday party and simply joined right in like he was one of the family. He was happy and smiling as I rushed to pick him up and wrapped him in a bear hug full of love and relief.

I went up to one of the women, frantic and gasping. I immediately explained what happened. I heard myself telling her the difference between 'the boys' and 'the babies'.

The look on her face was priceless.

When I was done with my long-winded explanation of how two otherwise-competent parents could leave a child behind for hours, she took a breath.

Then she let loose with her reprimand. 'How could you possibly forget your own child? We have been waiting here for ages to see who he belonged to. What happened? Where were you? What were you thinking?'

I was devastated. I apologised, shame-faced, and slunk back to my car knowing that we had messed up big-time.

But I also knew that these are the special challenges parents of twins face. Besides, we had gifted that woman with a story that she is probably still telling decades later. Now that I think of it, she should thank us!

In a similarly harrowing tale, my husband and I decided that we would take the kids away for the weekend. My sister-in-law

TWINS

had a lovely holiday flat that we borrowed for our weekend of family bliss. It was a major undertaking to take our four kids with all their bags, food, supplies and equipment. But the promise of a weekend away surrounded by sand, surf and parks was too alluring to resist. The only problem was that we got anything but quiet bliss.

Once we had arrived and got the children settled and the car unpacked, it started to get a bit chilly, so I turned on the heater. It was an old-style unit that sat on the floor near the wall and radiated out into the room. We turned on the television to entertain the kids for a bit while we finished getting unpacked.

With the chill leaving the indoor air and the kids settling, I decided to join James in the shower. Yes, it felt like a good idea at the time! The next thing we heard was a bloodcurdling scream and the word, 'Fire.'

My husband beat me getting out of the bathroom, but only by a second. I burst through the door and ran naked and barefoot into the living room to see the room in flames. The heater had been knocked over and ignited the curtains. I scooped up all four children and ran toward the door. My husband rushed to extinguish the fire, ripping curtains off their frames, and then stomping them out on the carpet. I found myself down the bottom of the stairwell, naked to the bone, holding my gorgeous babies and assuring them all was fine.

I'm sure the neighbours who witnessed the mayhem from the balcony are still talking about the naked lady and her fire dance.

After two sets of twins, we were blessed with a single birth, our youngest daughter. The other four think she is spoiled because she had so much of mum's attention without a twin sister or brother demanding half of my time.

It is interesting to watch her watch her older brothers and sister. I vividly remember one day when I was acutely aware of this. We went to a cafe and the boys were opening the sugar and pouring it out. I was frantically trying to get everyone to stop. I looked over at my daughter. She was sitting there watching her siblings behave like feral animals, thankful for her babycino and mummy moments while her siblings were all at school. The smirk of superiority on her face was priceless!

We spent a lot of time outdoors because it wasn't easy to be indoors with all the children. Everything was complicated and more difficult, from shopping to going to the amusement park. The juggling act of pushing a double stroller around a supermarket with four babies attracted jaw-dropping stares, applause and sympathy depending on that fine line between pleasure and pain.

They were especially rambunctious in the grocery store. I grew weary of little mishaps like broken eggs on the floor or a cereal box pulled open and scattered through the trolley.

Mostly, I was tired of constantly apologising to the people in line behind me as I tried to get my food and my brood through the check-out. There was no internet shopping at the time where I could order things to be conveniently delivered to my doorstep. If I wanted it, I had to go out and get it. Finally, I started to shop late at night because I could swan around the supermarket slowly and pretend I had my life all together.

Following 'the park incident', our youngest son Sam became an especially crafty escape artist and managed to get 'lost' on regular occasions. When I reflect on those frantic moments at the beach, the zoo and the shops, it still makes my heart race.

I often joked that he had delusions of grandeur, thinking that he could just venture off exploring without a care in the world. You can't plan for these random moments as they are unique to every child and every family. But there are some things you can do to be better prepared for the incredible and magical ride you are embarking on.

CHAPTER 23

LEARNED WISDOM

'Parenthood is about providing your kids solid foundations, unconditional love and wings to fly.'
Annie Gibbins

When we look back on raising our family, there is not much we would change. There were many moments where we felt ill prepared for the demands and responsibility, but we pushed through and became stronger and wiser throughout the roller-coaster journey that is twin parenting. When I look back on the magic moments, of which there are zillions, I know our love and ability was not measured by our age, titles or wealth; it was the attention and time we gave that mattered, and we gave that in abundance.

When embarking on raising the next generation there is no recipe book, blog or wise woman who can answer every question you may have. You will have to give yourself gold medals for endurance, resilience and negotiation, as your performance will be outstanding but not always appreciated or noticed. And that's okay, as parents around the world quietly salute you and wish you well.

You will survive the sleepless nights, breaking up fights, years of homework and extracurricular activities, school proms, teaching them to drive and waiting for them to come home from a night out with friends. And you will smile as you reflect back with love and admiration, as we do, on the amazing family you have created, nurtured, loved, protected, equipped and cherished.

You are truly blessed now and in the future. Memories are forever and the golden ones never fade. As parents of adult children, we now watch and guide them (when invited) as they navigate their own life journeys. Two of our sons are now married and we have two beautiful granddaughters to love, spoil and return to their parents when the need arises.

We get to be part of the lives our children build for themselves, and it is such a joy. We observe choices they make that occasionally surprise us and we accept them for who they are. We listen to their joys and struggles and are there to meet them wherever they are at.

We constantly learn from their unique personalities, perspectives, experiences, knowledge and skills. Although raised as a tribe, they are all different, and it's discovering and respecting these differences that matters. Above everything, the depth and consistency of our unconditional love for them all is at the centre of all family occasions, group chats, private moments and prayers.

That is enough.

It is always enough.

Your love is enough.

APPENDIX 1

STANDARD OBSTETRIC APPOINTMENT SCHEDULE

FIRST VISIT

- Confirmation that you are pregnant.
- Calculating how many weeks your pregnancy is and when your due date will be. You may be offered an ultrasound if the date is not clear.
- Blood pressure, height and weight.
- Medical and family history.
- A blood test, including checking your blood group and testing for anaemia, rubella immunity, hepatitis B, hepatitis C, syphilis, chlamydia and HIV.
- Urine test, to see if you have a bladder or urinary tract infection.
- Screening for Down syndrome.
- Cervical screening to check for human papillomavirus

(HPV) and/or any signs of cervical cancer.
- If at risk of vitamin D deficiency, a test for this may be offered.

As part of your check-up, you will usually also discuss with your doctor or midwife:

- Which medications you are taking.
- Whether you smoke or drink alcohol.
- Whether you would like an influenza vaccination.
- Which vitamin and mineral supplements you can take or should avoid.
- Antenatal care options available to you.
- Where you can get further information and antenatal classes.

19-20 WEEKS

- Blood pressure.
- Measuring your tummy (abdominal palpation) to check your babies' growth.
- Checking how your health is and if there are any problems.
- Ultrasound scan to check your babies' physical development, growth and any complications with your pregnancy. If you want to, during the ultrasound, you can find out the sex of the babies.

22 WEEKS

- Blood pressure.
- Measuring your tummy (abdominal palpation) to check your babies' growth.
- Checking how your health is and if you have any problems.

26-27 WEEKS

- Blood pressure.
- Measuring your tummy (abdominal palpation) to check your babies' growth.
- Checking how your health is and if you have any problems.
- Blood glucose tolerance test for diabetes.

28 WEEKS

- Blood pressure.
- Measuring your tummy (abdominal palpation) to check babies' growth.
- Checking how your health is and if you have any problems.
- Checking your babies' heartbeats and movements.
- Discussing your birth plan and going home with your babies.
- Blood test to check for anaemia and blood platelet levels.
- If your blood type is Rh negative, an anti-D immunoglobulin injection may be given.
- Pertussis (whooping cough) vaccination.
- Urine test, if you have signs of a urinary tract infection or raised blood pressure.

32 WEEKS

- Blood pressure.
- Measuring your tummy (abdominal palpation) to check your babies' growth.
- Checking how your health is and if you have any problems.
- Checking your babies' heartbeats and movements.
- Urine test, if you have signs of a urinary tract infection or raised blood pressure.

34-36 WEEKS

- Blood pressure.
- Measuring your tummy (abdominal palpation) to check your babies' growth.
- Checking how your health is and if you have any problems.
- Checking your babies' heartbeats and movements.
- Urine test, if you have signs of a urinary tract infection or raised blood pressure.
- Vaginal swab for group B streptococcus (GBS).
- If your blood type is Rh negative, a second anti-D immunoglobulin injection may be given.
- Assessing presentation (which way up your babies are) and station (how far down the babies' heads have moved into your pelvis).

38-39 WEEKS

- Blood pressure.
- Measuring your tummy (abdominal palpation) to check your babies' growth.
- Checking how your health is and if you have any problems.
- Checking your babies' heartbeats and movements.
- Urine test, if you have signs of a urinary tract infection or raised blood pressure.
- Assessing presentation and station.

APPENDIX 2

NEW BABY CHECKLIST

CLOTHING

- 16 Onesies – side snap.
- 16 Undershirts, side snap (short and/or long-sleeve should be based on the season or climate).
- 16 One-piece pyjamas (weight should be based on the season or climate).
- 4 Sleepers.
- 3-6 Sweaters or jackets (front button).
- 4-6 Dress-up outfits.
- 16 Pairs of socks or booties.
- 6 Hats (based on the season or climate).
- 4 Pairs of no-scratch mittens.
- 4 Fleece bunting suits (based on the season or climate).

NURSERY FURNITURE

- 2 Bassinets with insert.
- 2 Cribs.

- 2 Crib mattress, snug fitting, firm and flat.
- Rocking chair.
- Baby monitor.
- Nightlight.
- Dresser.
- Hamper.
- Changing table and pad.
- Diaper pail and liners.
- 2 Bouncers or swings.

BABIES' ROOM – ACCESSORIES

- 3-6 Waterproof mattress pads.
- 4-8 Crib sheets and crib blankets.
- 8-12 Receiving blankets or swaddles.
- 12-Dozen cloth diapers.
- 6-Dozen washcloths.
- Baby hangers.
- Baby gym, playpen or play mat, soft toys, books.
- Bassinet/crib mobile.
- Diaper cream and baby powder.
- Infant tub.
- Bath wraps.
- Hooded towels.
- Grooming kit.
- Night-light.

TRAVEL

- 3 Diaper bags with changing pads.
- 2 Car seats or carriers (car seats can double as carriers).
- 2 Back seat mirrors – one for each side of the car.
- Double pram/stroller.
- Travel crib.

FEEDING

- Bibs.
- Burp cloths.
- Nursing pillow.
- Baby bottles.
- Countertop drying rack.

APPENDIX 3

BIRTH PLAN TEMPLATE

Place of birth with address. First preference. Second preference.	*Reassess for each birth scenario (i.e. homebirth, birth centre, hospital, etc.).
Birth companions.	List your partner, doula, midwife, children, etc. Would you permit a student to be present?
Contact phone numbers.	Spouse/partner: Midwife: Doula: Doctor: Nearest hospital:

Induction/augmentation.	List your preferences: Artificial induction/augmentation. Membrane sweep. Natural induction methods (i.e. castor oil, herbs, homeopathy, lovemaking, meditation, aromatherapy, acupressure, etc.).
Environment.	List your preferences: Music. Chatter. Calm atmostphere. Lighting. Temperature.
First stage of labour.	List your preferences: Eating/drinking. Mobility. TENS machine. Entonox. Pethidine. Epidural. Water pool. Massage. Aromatherapy. Homeopathy. Hot/cold packs.

Fetal monitoring/vaginal examiations.	What method of monitoring do you prefer: electronic or doppler. State your preference regarding vaginal examinations.
Second stage of labour.	List your preferences: Position. Pushing. Touching babies' heads. Discovering the sex. Photos.
Assisted delivery.	List your preferences: Forceps. Ventouse. Episiotomy. Perennial massage. Hot compresses.
Cutting the cord.	List your preferences: How long would you like to wait after the birth before cutting the cords? Who would you like to cut them (i.e. your partner). Are you planning a lotus birth? Would you like to keep the placenta?

Third stage of labour.	List your preferences: Syntometrine. Syntocinon. Pulling on the cord. Herbs/homeopathy. Fundal pressure. Breastfeeding.
Fourth stage of labour (postpartum).	List your preferences: Bonding/skin-to-skin immediately after birth. Weighing/measuring, washing and dressing babies. When would you like to shower or bathe? When would you like to eat/drink?
Baby care.	List your preferences: Skin-to-skin contact. Breastfeeding. Pacifiers. Glucose water. Circumcision. Vitamin K. Vaccinations.

IN CASE OF AN EMERGENCY, CAESAREAN BIRTH OR SICK BABIES

Advocate – in an emergency, if I am unable to speak for myself, I would like for the following person to be my advocate.	State who you would like to advocate for you in the event that you are unable to speak for yourself (i.e. your partner, doula, midwife, etc.).

APPENDIX 4

SAFETY CHECKLIST

- Add floor padding to hard surfaces where babies might fall. (Puzzle piece pads are not recommended as your babies will quickly learn how to take them apart. You will be constantly putting them back together.)
- Outlet covers. Some countries like England have specialised covers that don't allow currents to run through the socket like outlets in the US do. But some outlets have switches that must be turned off. To be on the safe side, cover all outlets. Be sure to cover outdoor outlets as well.
- Baby gates. These are fantastic at placing barriers between babies and danger. But beware: a poorly built or poorly installed baby gate can actually cause injury while trying to prevent one. About five children in the US are injured daily in baby gate accidents. Most were under the age of two.

'Baby gates are essential safety devices for parents and caregivers, and they should continue to be used,' said Lara McKenzie, PhD, the study's co-author and a principal investigator in the Centre for Injury Research and Policy at

Nationwide Children's Hospital. 'It is important, however, to make sure you are using a gate that meets the voluntary safety standards and is the right type of gate for where you are planning to use it.'

Dr McKenzie recommends parents think of pressure-mounted gates as products that should only be used as room dividers or at the bottom of stairs because those kinds of gates are not designed to withstand much force and will not prevent a fall down stairs. For the top of the stairs, only gates that have hardware, which needs to be screwed into the wall or railing, will be strong enough to prevent a child from falling down the stairs.

nationwidechildren.org

- Window guards. Keeping kids from crawling out of windows is essential to safety. These window guards are easy to install and restrict how much the window can be opened.
- Secure furniture. Babies can be crushed when bookshelves and other furniture are not anchored to the wall. Furniture that can tip over should be secured. Be sure to check outdoor furniture as well.
- Remove all cords on window coverings. Cords on window blinds and curtains represent a serious choking hazard. Kids like to play with them but can get tangled up in them and strangle themselves. Be sure to check outdoor cords on awnings and other coverings.
- Remove heavy items from high places. TVs, for example, are often placed on high furniture. However, even if the furniture is well-anchored, a climber can knock a heavy item

down causing injury to themself or a sibling.
- Power strip covers. As you are thinking about covering those electric outlets, you should ensure that power strips are covered. Because power strips usually rest on the floor, outlet covers are not as effective. Ensure that the entire strip is in a safety box/cover.
- Zip-tie all cords. Cords on electronics are much like cords on window coverings when it comes to hazards in the home. Zip ties are excellent at both organising cords and ensuring that they are not hanging.
- Door latches. Invest in high-quality door latches to keep babies out of closets, cabinets, toilets, ovens and other places where they are likely to get hurt. Some are poor quality and can be easily defeated by smart babies. Invest in the ones that have the best safety rating.
- Corner bumpers. If you have ever rounded a corner and bumped your leg or stubbed your toe on a piece of furniture, you can imagine the damage a sharp corner can do to a baby. Install corner bumpers on all such furniture to protect little legs and heads.
- Baby-proof your guests. You may have heard the sad case of the puppy who died when a family member came over to visit and left her purse on the floor. The dog got curious and managed to get into a medicine bottle and died. Guests who come to visit should have a designated place (a locked closet) where they can put their belongings so that they do not introduce any dangers into your baby-proofed home.
- Post emergency numbers everywhere. It is not enough to have emergency numbers in the nursery or kitchen. They

should be in every room so that, in an emergency, you can reach help faster. When an accident occurs, every second matters. You don't want to have to run into a nearby room to get a phone number and leave a sick child alone in another room.

- Make believe you're a baby. This is a fun activity, but also a critical safety measure. Get down on your hands and knees and look at the world through your babies' eyes. What hazards do you see from that low? Are there loose nails, fabrics hanging under the couch, an ink pen that accidently rolled behind a table?

ABOUT THE AUTHOR
ANNIE GIBBINS

Starting her career as a registered nurse, Annie went on to become a health educationist, change management CEO and entrepreneur whilst raising her family of five, including two sets of twins born 26 months apart.

Annie Gibbins is a passionate and purpose-driven 'fempreneur', global women's empowerment coach, CEO, podcast host, speaker and number-one bestselling author.

Positioned as one of Australia's leading voices for women in leadership and founder of The Women's Business Incubator and

The Women's Business Tribe, Annie is a digital powerhouse helping women push the limits of what is truly possible.

As G100 Australia Country Chair – Equity & Equality, her passion for gender equality is unwavering when it comes to excelling the potential of the female workforce. Annie is driven by demolishing the glass ceiling and removing the invisible barriers to success that many women come up against in their business and life journey.

As the host of *Memoirs of Successful Woman*, Annie has interviewed hundreds of inspirational women worldwide. Her continuous portfolio of high-calibre podcast guests range from business leaders, entrepreneurs, humanitarians, athletes and the creators of startups on a mission.

With three university degrees under her belt and 20 years of executive change management experience, Annie is now a go-to inspirational global speaker. In 2020, she earned the distinguished 'Unsung Business Hero' title in recognition of her formidable courage, compassion, perseverance, conviction and selflessness when coaching women to thrive. Speaking at the World Economic Forum, Annie shared the importance of engagement with political, business and cultural leaders to shape global, regional and industry agendas.

As a keynote speaker at the 'Lady America Power: Barriers and Bias, The Status of Women in Leadership' in 2021, Annie shared the power behind unlocking the visibility of female entrepreneurs around the globe. This prestigious event celebrated women internationally, heralding the importance of women in leadership.

Global brand, Hoinser Group, dedicated to promoting outstanding individuals in business throughout Europe, Africa, Asia,

UAE and USA, invited Annie to their collective as an honourable member, elevating her influence tenfold.

Annie has graced covers and written articles for books and magazines including *1 Habit Leadership, I am Woman Global, Lady Speaker Power, Success, Hoinser, W, CIO Times,* and *MO2VATE Magazine.* She was named Top Women's Change Maker and Global Goodwill Ambassador in 2021.

THE BACKSTORY

After graduating with a Diploma of Health Science and working as a registered nurse, Annie's thirst for professional development continued, leading her to complete a Master of Education. Identified as a leader in the health education sector, Annie was coined a leader to watch. As a recognised businesswoman and thought leader, Annie was determined to become a successful CEO.

With only 17% of Australian CEOs being women at the time, Annie was determined to head a company in this prestigious role. With her tribe of children to raise, it was an ambitious dream. After completing the Australian Institute of Company Directors and Lean Six Sigma qualifications, Annie landed her first CEO position in 2011.

For over 12 years Annie held senior executive positions and gained extensive C-suite experience and change management success by leading national and international health organisations through transformational change and success. Annie is now engaged as a regular keynote speaker on strategic growth, organisational excellence, gender equality, leadership and success.

Her many professional accolades gained over 30 years across health, education, corporate, NFP and charity sectors drive her to inspire and empower women across the globe to achieve success in business and life.

Becoming Annie the Biography of a Curious Woman inspires women to set the bar high to achieve success, balance and happiness on their terms.

Women from around the world can access Annie's atomic energy, skill and wisdom through her transformational coaching programs. Power, freedom and confidence gained from her decades of business and life experience quickly shift them from where they now are to where they dream to be.

Signature programs incxude:

- The Women's Start up Incubator
- The Women's Scale up Incubator
- The Business Domination Incubator
- Life by Design

Reach out to Annie:

- anniegibbins.com
- womensbiztribe.com
- womensbizincubator.com

REFERENCES

- Twins Research Australia
- todaysparent.com/baby/newborn-care/real-life-parenting-hacks-for-raising-twins
- seattlepi.com/seattlenews/article/UW-study-fetal-alcohol-syndrome-twins-siblings-13550104.php
- health.harvard.edu/blog/study-no-connection-between-drinking-alcohol-early-in-pregnancy-and-birth-problems-201309106667
- livescience.com/identical-twins-dont-share-all-dna.html
- smithsonianmag.com/science-nature/brief-history-twin-studies-180958281
- apa.org/monitor/apr04/herit
- sciencealert.com/becoming-parents-makes-us-25-percent-less-environmentally-friendly-says-new-report
- recalls.gov
- productsafety.gov.au/recalls
- Australian Private Hospitals Association (Private hospital service provision)
- Australian Government (Health)

- Australian Institute of Health and Welfare (Overview of public and private hospitals)
- Australian Medical Association (Private patients public hospitals)
- NSW Health (Going to hospital)
- MyDr (Australian health system: how it works)
- en.wikipedia.org/wiki/Cholestasis
- hopkinsmedicine.org/health/conditions-and-diseases/staying-healthy-during-pregnancy/twin-pregnancy-answers-from-maternal-fetal-medicine-specialist

www.ingramcontent.com/pod-product-compliance
Lightning Source LLC
Chambersburg PA
CBHW020321010526
44107CB00054B/1925